Orchids for the South

Orchids for the South

Jack Kramer

TAYLOR TRADE PUBLISHING
Lanham • New York • Dallas • Boulder• Toronto • Oxford

Published by Taylor Trade Publishing
An imprint of The Rowman & Littlefield Publishing Group, Inc.
4501 Forbes Boulevard, Suite 200
Lanham, Maryland 20706

Distributed by National Book Network

Page ii: *One of the wonderful Vuylstekeara hybrids.*
(William Shaban)

Page vi: *Cypripedium Wineva Superior shows the large classic
form of its parents, C. Winston and C. Bourneva, made in 1977.*
(Bob Jones)

Designed by Hespenheide Design

Library of Congress Cataloging-in-Publication Data
Kramer, Jack, 1927–
    Orchids for the South / Jack Kramer
    p. cm.
    ISBN 0–87833–857–8
    1. Orchid culture—Southern States. 2. Orchids—Southern
    States. 3. Orchids—Southern States—Pictorial works.
    I. Title.
    SB409.5.U6K73 1994
    635.9'3415'0975—dc20   94–4992
                         CIP

Printed in the United States of America

Contents

Preface

Thirty years ago I grew orchids in Chicago, Illinois, with some success and wrote the first book in the United States devoted entirely to growing species orchids at home, *Growing Orchids at Your Windows.* When I and some of my orchid collection moved from Illinois to northern California, a temperate climate, however, I quickly discovered that my cool-growing orchids did not grow well there. Five years ago I came to southern Florida and shipped some of my orchids; most did not respond to the warm temperatures and humidity. I soon started to grow mainly warmth-loving orchids (with the exception of a few species), selecting plants carefully. Success! The plants thrived.

Talking with orchid hobbyists in the South and attending local orchid society meetings, I found that most of the orchids grown were Vandas, Phalaenopses, Cattleyas, and Dendrobiums. Where were the graceful Epidendrums, the colorful Oncidiums, scented Aerides, unusual Stanhopeas, and other warm-growing orchids mainly from countries whose climate paralleled ours in the South?

In *Orchids for the South,* I discuss orchids that thrive in Alabama, Arkansas, the southern portions of the Carolinas, Florida, Georgia, Louisiana, Mississippi, Oklahoma, Tennessee, and Texas. These are plants that grow with us and for us. The cool growers, such as Odontoglossums and Coelogynes, I leave to the climes of Minnesota, Illinois, and other northern states.

Simply put, I have found that orchids from warm climates prefer to be grown in warmth, those from cold climates, coolness. I have asked orchid hybridists why this is so, and they say it has to do with the genes of the plant—simple inheritance.

To grow orchids successfully in the South, I have found it a matter of selecting the right plants for the right climate, then applying appropriate culture. This is the difference between failure and success. So, whether you are growing orchids in a greenhouse, on a windowsill, in a lath house, or in a landscape (and there are *many* orchids that grow well *in* Southern gardens!), here are more than 200 plants for your consideration. Join me and don't fight Mother Nature. Work with her. The rewards can be beautiful orchids.

—JJK

Author's Notes

• Orchid nomenclature is never constant; name changes are occasionally made. For the most part I have used the botanical names currently in use in catalogs and by growers. By the time this book goes to press, there may be further changes in some orchid names.

• Thousands of hybrid orchids are registered yearly, and new Cattleyas,

Phalaenopses, and plants of other genera come and go. Old favorites are replaced by new hybrids. For growing hybrids I have tried to suggest plants that have withstood the test of time and are available. And too, the hybrids I have selected are my favorites, most of which I have personally grown. You may have favorites of your own. An omission of a specific hybrid is often a matter of space and my own personal preference.

• Some of the orchids referred to in this book or appearing in nature may be poisonous. Any person, particularly a novice gardener, should exercise care in handling plants. The publisher and the author accept no responsibility for any damage or injury resulting from the use of, ingestion of, or contact with any orchid discussed in this book.

Acknowledgments

I wish to thank the many friends and orchid-growing folks I have met since my move to Florida, with special gratitude to the following people who allowed me to photograph on their premises: Jerry Manning, who has a fabulous orchid collection in a screened enclosure; Jack Hild, who grows beautiful Cattleyas and Dendrobiums in a lath house; the people at the Naples Beach Hotel, especially Ursula Malone, who tends their collection.

I must include outdoor garden enthusiasts George Evans and Lou Szabo for showing me their orchids growing outdoors. Thanks also to the many people who have called me to ask questions about warmth-loving orchids. I am sure I gained more information from them than I gave.

I also wish to thank the Marie Selby Botanical Gardens in Sarasota, Gene Hausermann of Hausermann Orchids of Villa Park, Illinois and Hermann Pigors of Oak Hill Gardens in Dundee, Illinois. And, as always, my thanks to the American Orchid Society and Jim Watson.

Lastly, thanks for the beautiful climate of the South, where warm days and ample sun make it possible to provide a home for some of the most beautiful orchids that grow worldwide.

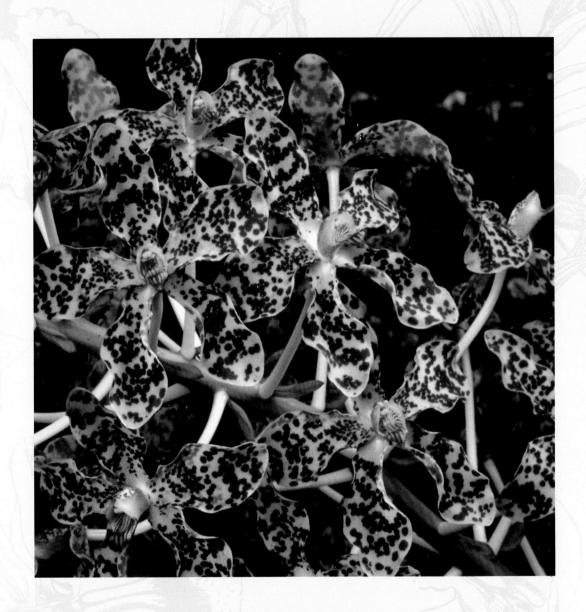

Grammatophyllum scriptum
*is an unusual orchid with brown flowers,
many to a stem. It hardly
resembles the orchids we know.*

CHAPTER ONE

The Orchid World

More than 35,000 wild species of orchids grow throughout the world, from Alaska to the Himalayas. Yes, even in Alaska—not all or even very many orchids thrive only in the hot and steamy areas of the world, contrary to what we have believed for many, many decades.

Consider the following range of orchids around the globe. The Pleione often breaks through the snow to bloom in Japan. Some Grammatophyllum orchids grow to giant heights in the torrid African jungles. And the lands of South America support thousands of species, even in the high Andes Mountains. All these orchids, regardless of their climatic preferences, need one important condition: good air circulation, because few orchids can grow in a stagnant atmosphere.

Most orchids dwell in treetops, leading arboreal lives high above the ground; these plants are found mainly in the tropical rain forests at cooler elevations from 3,000 to 4,500 feet. Other orchids, such as the Paphiopedilums (Cypripediums), grow on the ground. Still others, such as the Coelogynes and Restrepias, thrive at still cooler heights of 8,000 feet. Thus, orchids grow in three different climatic situations: warmth, intermediate temperatures, and coolness (45°F at night).

Early growers were unaware of this fact because orchids were then so rare and popular that knowing the source of an orchid was as valuable as having a treasure map; most collectors never divulged the exact regions plants came from. As a result, early growers assumed that all orchids grew in the exotic hot and humid regions plied by the collectors' ships. Local growers and hobbyists decided that all orchids needed excessive warmth and humid conditions. This fallacy lingered for many years, causing the deaths of thousands of cool- and temperate-growing orchids being raised in sealed glass houses. After trial and error, growers realized that

Cypripedium reginae,
an endangered species, is a
terrestrial orchid that grows in
shaded, somewhat temperate
conditions.
(Hermann Pigors)

Vanda 'Evening Glow', a
hybrid, has its origin in India,
where there are defined seasons
of rain and dry months.

Opposite: A very old genus, the
favorite Oncidiums never fail
to please with wands of bright
yellow and brown flowers.

orchid culture involves the three different climatic conditions: warm, moderate, and cool.

WHERE ORCHIDS COME FROM

The tropics are home to many of the orchids that can be cultivated in the South. Our temperatures of 80° to 90°F by day and ten to fifteen degrees less at night suit an array of orchids originally from parts of Central America, South America, Asia, and Africa. These areas have uniformly warm days, with slightly cooler nights; temperatures do not vary much from season to season. These regions also have definite dry and rainy seasons that more or less correspond to the winters and summers we have here; somewhat dry in the winter but quite rainy in the summer. Numerous tropical orchids will grow in less than optimal conditions, but they positively thrive in their native type of atmosphere, which the climate of our Southern areas duplicates.

Some (but not all) of the orchids that prefer moderate conditions will also thrive in the South because they can adjust to imperfect circumstances. Cymbidiums, cool-growing orchids, never before thrived in the South, but a warmth-tolerant Cymbidium has been developed for the Southern states.

Most orchids are grown indoors in greenhouses, garden rooms, solariums, or sunrooms. However, in the climates of Zones 8, 9, 10, and 11 (climate zones established by the United States Department of Agriculture), species that specifically prefer the outdoors,

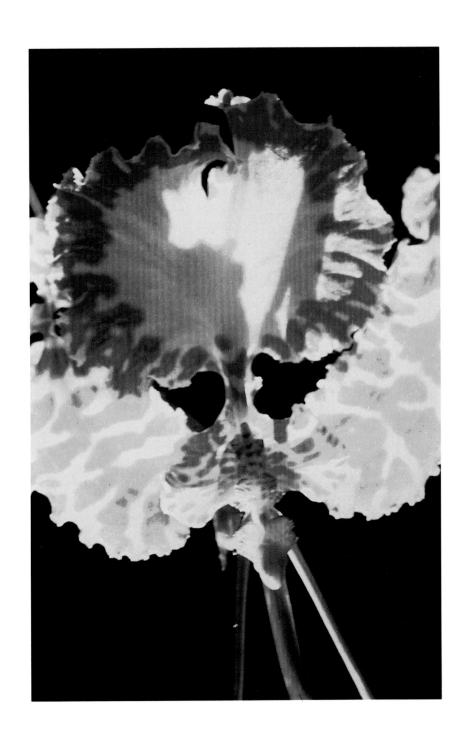

including the Epidendrums, the free-blooming Oncidiums, the stunning Vandas, and Ascocentrums, thrive.

If you are wealthy and persistent and have the right heating and cooling equipment, you can obviously accommodate all types of orchids: cool, warm, or temperate growers. But doing so will be expensive and require a great deal of time and effort. And even the cool-growing orchids may not respond well in a warm area to artificial heating and cooling; somehow orchids grown inside under simulated conditions still respond to their inherent genetic natural characteristics.

ORCHID FACTS AND FANCY

It has been more than 100 years since people began cultivating orchids, but certain misconceptions about the plants persist even today. First, even though orchids use tree branches as support, they are *not* parasitic, because they derive no nourishment from the host trees. Another myth is that orchids are difficult to grow; actually, they can be grown as easily as houseplants. Finally, contrary to a third myth, orchids do not have to be grown in greenhouses.

Most orchids are easy to grow because their pseudobulbs (thickened portion of stem) store water and nutrients, which helps the plants if we forget to water them. Orchids do need a buoyant atmosphere of circulating air, but they neither want nor need excessive humidity or scorching sunlight. Indeed, such conditions will quickly kill orchids.

An advantage of orchids is that insects rarely attack them because most orchid species have leaves that are just too tough for bugs. Insects will seek to obtain easier fodder. And disease is seldom a problem for orchids because healthy, mature plants are very resistant to bacterial infection.

Years ago, many orchids were imported, but this practice has been stopped—most countries do not allow their orchids to be exported, and those countries that do permit exportation have very strict quotas. Ninety-five percent of all orchids now being sold in the United States are hybridized in laboratories. Any bad features are being bred out, leaving orchids of superior quality.

The original species orchids of years ago are no longer available from their native countries. Their offspring, though, are being sold as growers continue to propagate the species by seed or cloning. Examples include *Brassia verrucosa* and *Ansellia africana*, both wonderful warm-growing orchids.

CLIMATE AND ORCHIDS

When I first started writing about orchids some years ago, I advocated growing those orchids that come from areas with temperatures and conditions similar to the climate in your specific region. Making the right selection of orchids means you will be able to grow the plants successfully with minimal care. Quite simply, the plants are used to the climate.

It is interesting to compare the weather statistics of various Southern cities with the temperatures for parts of the world where many orchids came from originally. You will note the similarities.

✐PRING ✐EATHER IN THE ✐OUTH AND THE ✐ROPICS

		TEMPERATURE[1]		HUMIDITY[1]
		HIGH	LOW	
Southern United States[2]				
	Asheville, NC	69	43	67
	Atlanta, GA	73	50	62
	Birmingham, AL	75	50	66
	Charleston, SC	76	53	70
	Charlotte, NC	72	48	60
	Dallas, TX	77	55	66
	Jackson, MS	77	53	71
	Jacksonville, FL	80	56	71
	Louisville, KY	68	44	63
	Memphis, TN	73	52	64
	Miami, FL	82	68	68
	Mobile, AL	78	58	71
	New Orleans, LA	79	59	74
	Norfolk, VA	68	48	64
	Oklahoma City, OK	72	49	62
	Tampa, FL	82	61	70
Tropics[3]				
Africa	Madagascar	100	55	
	Tanzania	93	64	
Asia	Bangkok, Thailand	106	52	
	Bombay, India	100	56	
	Borneo	97	69	
	Burma	101	50	
	Java	96	64	
	Manila, Philippines	101	58	
	New Guinea	98	68	
	Singapore	97	66	
	Sri Lanka	97	62	
Central and South America	Caracas, Venezuela	91	45	
	Guatemala City, Guatemala	90	41	
	Iquitos, Peru (on the Amazon)	88	54	
	Rio de Janeiro, Brazil	102	52	
	San Jose, Costa Rica	94	47	

[1]Daily averages for month. These numbers vary, of course, from year to year.

[2]January temperatures range about 15 degrees lower, but humidity remains about the same. Only in Asheville, Louisville, and Nashville do temperatures drop below freezing (32°F).

[3]Humidity in these places varies from 60 to 90 percent, depending upon the city.

Here is an example of
the hybridist's art: a handsome
multicolored flower:
Vuylstekeara Shirley Pozzato.

(McLellan Orchids)

CHAPTER TWO

How Orchids Grow

Terrestrial orchids grow in the ground like other plants. Some orchids tenaciously hug the sides of mountains for survival. But the majority of orchid species are arboreal, meaning that they cling to trees. These are epiphyte orchids, *epi* meaning "on" and *phyte* meaning "plant."

Orchids do not derive any nourishment from the host plant or tree; they grow where they can find a foothold. If a tree is not handy, orchids will endure life on a fallen log, a roof, or even some other plant. Through the centuries, the orchids, with nature's help, literally have climbed the trees and so have strong roots. This network of roots forms a catch basin for dead leaves and insects, twigs, and dust. This miscellaneous matter is dissolved by rain and furnishes nutrients for the plant. The roots are also fashioned to absorb any available moisture from the air.

Orchids belong to the flowering plant family of monocotyledons. They bear a single seed leaf (cotyledon) upon germination; additional leaves are then produced from the center of the stem, passing outward. True bark is absent, and leaves usually have parallel veins. Orchids exhibit two types of growth patterns. The sympodial orchids (for example, Cattleyas) bear new growth each year from the base of the preceding growth. This new growth produces flowers and makes its own roots; the cycle repeats itself over and over. In the monopodial growth pattern, one stem grows taller each year, and no new shoot is produced from the base of the plant. Vandas are monopodial-growing orchids. The flower spikes and roots grow from the root axils.

FLOWERS

The tremendous variety of flower forms and sizes makes orchids unique in the plant world. Generally, orchid flowers are about 3 to 4 inches in diameter. Some miniature orchids, however, such as the Bulbophyllums and Cirrhopetalums, bear flowers only $1/32$

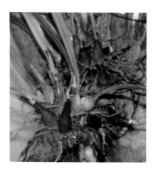

While many orchids, such as this small Epidendrum, grow on tree limbs, they derive no nourishment from the host.

inch in diameter, while other orchids, such as the Sobralias, flaunt flowers 7 to 9 inches across. The flowers may be single, in tight clusters, or in groups of 50 to 100 to a stem. Some orchids bear an erect flower stem, but dozens of others bear long, pendant stems adorned with beautiful flowers.

The colors of orchid flowers are stunning. Originally pink, white, and lavender flowers predominated, but now, as a result of hybridization, flowers run the gamut of the rainbow, including blue. The white and lavender orchids are still favorites, but many orchids are yellow, such as the famous Dendrobiums from India. A few orchids even masquerade as black, such as *Coelogyne pandurata* (the color is really a very dark green).

Shapes and sizes vary, too. Orchid flowers are great mimics. Some, like the Masdevallias, resemble small kites. The fanciful Catasetums look like birds in flight. Anguloas, a group of orchids from Colombia, display tulip-shaped flowers. Also distinctive are the Nun Orchid (*Phaius*), the Spider Orchid (*Brassia*) and the popular Moth Orchid (*Phalaenopsis*).

Most people can recognize the popular Cattleya flower on sight, but the flowers of the Gongoras, Stanhopeas, or Grammato-

Vandas show the monopodial type growth, one stem growing taller each year. Plants are easily propagated by removing the top portion of the plant and growing it as a new plant.

phyllums look like anything but those of an orchid; they are completely different in appearance, more bizarre than beautiful. There is truly an amazing diversification in orchid flower forms.

The fragrance of orchids is another factor that surprises people. Most orchids have scents strong enough to rival roses. *Brassavola nodosa* has a heavenly, gardenia-like fragrance, and the Galeandras have a hawthorn scent. Most white Cattleyas have a strong fragrance, and the Lycastes emit a cinnamon aroma. The Stanhopeas fill a room with a medicinal-like menthol odor.

In most flowers of various other plants, the stamens, anthers, pistil, and stigma are easy to see, but in orchids the stamen and the stigma are contained within the column of the flower.

Like the flowers of other plants, orchid flowers have sepals and petals, three of each. One petal is usually larger than the others and is called the lip. It is the most conspicuous part of the flower and can assume a variety of shapes, lobed, divided, spurred, slipper-shaped (as in the Paphiopedilums), trumpet-shaped, twisted, or curved and with various appendages. The structure of the lip may vary considerably, but its prime purpose is to assist in the fertilization of the flower. The flower of an orchid, no matter how beautiful we think it is, is actually a landing pad for an insect that will pollinate the plant.

ℒEAVES

Most orchid foliage is unattractive, usually hard, succulent, and broad, as in the

Cattleyas. In genera such as the Epidendrums and in some mule-type Oncidiums, the leaves are more cactuslike than one can imagine. It is difficult for insects to dine on orchid leaves because they are too tough; the insects look elsewhere for food. However, some orchids, including the Cymbidiums and many Oncidiums, have somewhat standard leaves of medium texture. A few orchids, such as the Catasetums and Phaiuses, have papery-thin leaves. Very few orchids have many leaves; they have single leaves, such as the pencil-like and cactuslike leaves in *Scuticaria* and *Brassavola nodosa*.

Some orchids, such as the Macodes and Anoechtochiluses, are grown only for their outstanding leaves, which compete with Rex begonias for beauty. These jewel orchids, as

Haemeria discolor from India is primarily grown for its maroon-colored foliage, but here the magnitude of its flowers excels.

they are usually called, have deep maroon, velvety leaves. Haemerias, also in this class, look like beautiful tapestries.

Seasonal Bloom

Nowhere in the plant world is there a group of plants that offers such an array of bloom throughout the year as orchids. Some orchid plants bloom in the spring, others in the summer, a majority in the autumn, and many in the winter. Generally, orchids bloom once a year, but the more recent hybrids offer flowers twice a year because of the mixed parentage.

With careful selection it is possible with only a dozen plants to have orchids blooming all year (see Appendices for suggestions). Outside, orchids for the spring and summer months will bloom with hundreds of flowers almost throughout the two seasons. Such orchids include the Epidendrums and Oncidiums; dozens of species with yellow to lilac flowers are available for growing outdoors where temperatures do not drop below 45°F.

Common Names

Common orchid names are often associated with animals or insects (for example, Butterfly Orchid, Moth Orchid) because the shape of the flower resembles a particular insect or part of an animal. Orchid names may also have religious connotations, most so named because of their flower shapes: *Peristeria elata* is the Holy Ghost Orchid; *Lycaste skinneri* v. *virginalis* is the White Nun Orchid; and *Epidendrum radicans* is the Crucifix Orchid. *Oncidium tigrinum*, though, is the Flower of the Dead because it blooms on All Souls' Day

and is used to decorate graves. The loveliest name is the Moon Orchid (*Phalaenopsis amabilis*), whose blooms last longer than a moon, the term for a month in Java.

Orchid Hybrids

Recently, when a yellow Cattleya was created to tolerate 40°F or lower outdoor temperatures, the event made the national news. Hybridization creates flowers and plants that have more desirable traits: more floriferousness, better flower color, more frequent blooms, and so on.

More hybrids have been produced in the orchid family than in any other. The process of transferring the pollen from one orchid to the stigma of another to create an orchid with the best characteristics of each parent began about 1869. John Dominy, the grower at the Veitch nursery at Exeter, England, used *Paphiopedilum* (*Cypripedium*) *barbatum* and

Oncidium papilio is called the butterfly orchid because its flowers fly on wiry stems in the slightest breeze. Flowers appear one after another over a period of about six weeks.

Opposite: The Cattleya is a sympodial orchid, bearing a new growth each year from the preceding growth.

(A. R. Addkison)

Oncidium Sharry Baby is one of the new Oncidiums bringing red color to the genus; this one grows luxuriantly in warm climates.

villosum to create long-lasting flowers on tall stems. The first Paphiopedilum hybrid was named *harrisianum* in honor of Dr. Jon Harris, a surgeon who first suggested to Dominy the feasibility of mixing plants.

To see what happens when certain plants are crossed with other plants, let's consider the basic Cattleya. The wild or species Cattleyas, such as *C. aclandiae* and *C. skinneri,* usually have small flowers with a small lip but excellent colors. By adding into the mix some *Brassavola digbyana,* a plant with a massive fringed lip, the hybridists were able to create a Cattleya with a beautiful ruffled lip.

Then the breeders decided to insert some Laelia lineage because many species of Laelias have large flowers. Large Cattleyas with large lips were produced; these hybrids are called Brassolaeliocattleyas. Then more vivid coloring was desired, such as red, so Sophronitis, plants with vivid red flowers, was added to the mix, eventually producing the red Cattleyas called Potinaras.

Within these four genera of Laelia, Brassavola, Cattleya, and Sophronitis, most of the Cattleya hybrids have been developed. Crosses between Epidendrums and Cattleyas have also been made, producing

Epicattleyas, small plants with multiple flower heads.

Extensive hybridization has been done with other genera such as Odontoglossums, Oncidiums, Brassias, Cochliodas, and Miltonias. However, not all crosses are outstanding; the various expert orchid societies decide which ones are. When an outstanding cross does occur, it is cloned (explained in a following section), so that thousands of plants can be made available to the public. Each plant is an exact genetic replica of the parent. Growers with stellar crosses can demand high prices for their work.

The breeding of hybrids has satisfied many demands, including superior flowers for market and orchids for warmer temperatures. Today, a primary reason for hybridization is conservation. Two clones of the same species are bred with each other. Thus, the species can be propagated in nurseries, allowing hobbyists to enjoy the many endangered species and, more importantly, guaranteeing the availability of the plants.

✑ NOMENCLATURE

The nomenclature for hybrids can be confusing. For example, what does Blc. Acapana 'Miles' HCC/AOS (Lc. Grande × Greenheart) mean? Blc. stands for Brassolaeliocattleya; Acapana is the hybrid name; 'Miles' is a selected clone or varietal name, denoting a single seed-grown individual. HCC means the plant was awarded the Highly Commended Certificate; AOS denotes an American Orchid Society winner (AM would denote Award of Merit). Lc. Grande × Greenheart is the lineage.

Brassolaeliocattleya Rising Sun: Here is a fine example of the three-way cross producing excellent yellow flowers.

Here is a hybridist's efforts at producing a white Cattleya. The results are quite rewarding.

Odontocidium Tiger Butter 'Yummy' is a fine orchid despite its Yummy name. The plant bears the typical yellow-and-brown Oncidium flowers—but larger.
(William Shaban)

the plant is from the genus Lycaste, and the species is *aromatica*. However, if you hybridize this plant with other Lycaste species, the resulting hybrid might be Lycaste 'Amber Gold.'

Orchid Abbreviations

Alcra.	Aliceara
Ascda.	Ascocenda
Asp.	Aspasia
B.	Brassavola
Bak.	Bakerara
Bc.	Brassocattleya
Blc.	Brassolaeliocattleya
Bllra.	Beallara
Bro.	Broughtonia
Brs.	Brassia
Brsdm.	Brassidium
Burr.	Burrageara
Bwna.	Brownara
C.	Cattleya
Cda.	Cochlioda
Colm.	Colmanara
Ctna.	Cattleytonia
Cym.	Cymbidium
Den.	Dendrobium
Dgmra.	Degarmoara
Dtps.	Doritaenopsis
Epi.	Epidendrum
Fgtra.	Forgetara
L.	Laelia
Lc.	Laeliocattleya
McLna.	MacLellanara
Milt.	Miltonia
Mpsa.	Milpasia
Mtad.	Miltada
Mtdm.	Miltonidium
Mtssa.	Miltassia
Oda.	Odontioda

The Royal Horticultural Society's *Sander's List of Orchid Hybrids* is the internationally recognized authority. The name and description of a flower and its color in this list stay the same for everywhere in the world, to ensure that anyone can get the exact plant desired.

Each hybrid group contains many different clones. Each clone has a name, called a cultivar. These names are always within single quotation marks to distinguish one clone (or variety) from others, such as 'Miles.'

Species names are not as complicated because there is no lineage to work from. For example, *Lycaste aromatica* means that

Odcdm.   Odontocidium
Odm.   Odontoglossum
Odtna.   Odontonia
Onc.   Oncidium
Paph.   Paphiopedilum
Phal.   Phalaenopsis
Pot.   Potinara
S.   Sophronitis
Slc.   Sophrolaeliocattleya
V.   Vanda
Vuyl.   Vuylstekeara
Wils.   Wilsonara

Award and Society Abbreviations

AM   Award of Merit
AOS   American Orchid Society
BM   Bronze Medal
CBM   Certificate of Botanical Merit
CCM   Certificate of Cultural Merit
CR   Certificate of Recognition
FCC   First Class Certificate
GM   Gold Medal
HCC   Highly Commended Certificate
HOS   Honolulu Orchid Society
JOGA   Japanese Orchid Growers
        Association
JOS   Japan Orchid Society
ODC   Orchid Digest Corporation
RHS   Royal Horticultural Society
RHT   Royal Horticultural Society of
        Thailand
SFOS   South Florida Orchid Society
SM   Silver Medal
5WOC   Fifth World Orchid Conference
7WOC   Seventh World Orchid
        Conference

8WOC   Eighth World Orchid Conference
11WOC   Eleventh World Orchid
        Conference

Cloning

Meristem culture, or cloning, is a miraculous process. The apical meristem (the point where plant tissue grows quickly) is separated from the base of a developing young growth within a plant. This tiny shoot is carefully dissected and placed in a liquid medium in a sterile flask. The flask is then placed on a revolving wheel, or agitator; the constant motion inhibits formation of a growing shoot or root. Instead, the tiny meristem cell multiplies into many protocorms, or embryos, that are then divided. The process can be done repeatedly, thus creating a large number of plants that are exact genetic replicas of the parent. The process is exacting and must be done very carefully and under sterile conditions. These plants are then replanted and grown on as seedlings.

The growth habit and flower color will exactly duplicate those of the mother plant, and the mericlones (the new plants) will flower each year at the same time the mother plant bloomed, which is a vital factor in the cut flower industry. Meristemming has reduced the price of top-quality orchids, making the very best plants available to and affordable for almost everyone. Meristemming is also a boon to conservation because it helps prevent the extinction of certain species.

*The signs of a healthy plant
are firm green leaves and
floriferousness; this yellow hybrid
Cattleya is worth a purchase.*

CHAPTER THREE

Buying Orchids

Orchids today are sold mainly as house-plants, to people who use the plants for interior enjoyment and decoration and to die-hard orchid enthusiasts—collectors and amateur growers—who cultivate orchids as a hobby. At one time, orchids were so plentiful that they could be purchased from numerous suppliers, such as mail-order houses, commercial nurseries, and discount stores such as Kmart. Now, however, because of stricter conservation regulations concerning the removal of orchids from their native habitats, the increasing popularity of orchids in this country, and the huge quantities of orchids American wholesalers have been selling abroad to enthusiastic collectors, demand is driving up the price of orchids. Thus, you must know just where and how to find good orchids at affordable prices.

It is now difficult to obtain native species of orchids, but because of the work of hybridists through the years and the success of cloning, many orchids are available at reasonable cost, say $25 to $30 for a mature Cattleya, for example. You can also buy seedlings in 4-inch pots for $10 or $15 (these plants will not bloom for about 2 years). The advantage of seedlings is that you can actually grow the plant to maturity yourself, which provides immense satisfaction as you bring the plant into bloom. The disadvantage is that you never know just what you are getting because you cannot see a flower. Mature plants usually are sold while in bud or in flower, so you have a good idea of what you are buying.

The latest hybrid costs more than an already-known plant, as much as $100 a

When buying plants look for color and form. This hybrid Cattleya is excellent in both respects. It is Slc. George Hausermann 'York'.
(Hausermann Orchids)

plant. However, once newly introduced hybrids have been in circulation for a year or two, the prices drop considerably as newer hybrids appear on the market.

Beware of orchids packaged in cellophane bags or in bubble packs and sold at very low prices. These cheap orchids are too young to survive and invariably die after a few months. They are years from blooming and require infinite care to bring into bloom. Also avoid the tiny orchid plants people bring back from places like Hawaii. Orchids are not indigenous to Hawaii; they were brought there and then thrived because of the amenable climate.

ℒ𝓮𝓁𝓮𝒸𝓉𝒾𝓸𝓃

When buying orchids, how do you distinguish a healthy orchid from a sick one? First, avoid a plant with limp foliage, no root activity, or signs of insect and disease dam-

age (small pits, scars, soft areas, and streaking of color darker than that of the leaves). If possible, select a plant that has a new lead (new growth) starting from previous growth. Inspect the bulbs of the bulbous-type orchids; they should be plump and firm, never soft or mushy, characteristics which can indicate rot.

Suppliers sell plants in pots or bare-root. Mail-order suppliers use plastic containers because clay pots weigh too much for shipping. Bare-root orchids are less expensive than potted ones and, if potted properly upon arrival, will survive and thrive. Orchids in bloom cost slightly more than those not yet in bud, but the extra expense is worth it because you can see the exact flower the plant will eventually bear.

𝒮𝒽𝒾𝓅𝓅𝒾𝓃𝓰 𝑀𝓮𝓉𝒽𝓸𝒹𝓈

If an orchid outlet is located near you, by all means buy plants there. If you are not near a local supplier, you can purchase beautiful orchids from the hundreds of reputable mail-order suppliers. These companies publish their own catalogs several times a year. Shipping can now be done almost year-round, except during subzero and very hot weather. Packing is much improved from that of a few years ago; various packing materials ensure safe arrival of your plants (even those in bud) in a few days.

Mail-order suppliers can ship your plants via various carriers, depending mainly on the mileage and how fast you want your plants. Federal Express, United Parcel Service, and the United States Postal

Left: A typical nursery where Cattleyas abound; it is always best to buy plants locally if possible so you see what you are actually purchasing.

Below: Another local nursery where you can buy plants; most mature Cattleyas cost about $25; Dendrobiums and Epidendrums about $20.

Service offer express (overnight) or 2-day service, but all three carriers have size limitations. Fast shipping methods can be expensive, and you usually must pick up the plants at the airport or pay a private hauling company to pick them up and deliver them to you. Both UPS and the Postal Service do offer slower and cheaper methods: UPS will ship ground; the Postal Service ships by priority rate (first class) or third class. If you are far from the mail-order supplier but are not in a hurry to receive your plants, rail is a very inexpensive and reliable shipping method. There are box size limitations, so check with carriers for specific sizes acceptable.

Wilsonara Celle speaks of beauty.
While not a typical warm-growing
orchid, it does with some coddling
respond in warm climates.

(William Shaban)

CHAPTER FOUR

Growing and Caring for Orchids Indoors

Once, all orchids were grown in sealed greenhouses because they were wild species from tropical rain forests, and it was assumed that plants away from the tropics had to be grown in similar situations. Now we know that orchids come from many different climatic areas of the world. Improved home heating and cooling systems make temperature control somewhat easier today; indoor lighting and large expanses of glass allow more light into homes, too. Thus, any indoor area can accommodate some orchid.

Maintaining proper humidity, temperature, and ventilation in the home for plants is not a problem if you select orchids that will adapt to your growing conditions. Humidity may fluctuate from 20 to 50 percent in the home depending on outside weather and the time of the year; it may be more humid in the summer than the winter, for example. Most orchids grow satisfactorily at about 70 percent humidity, a prevalent

figure in most warm states. And because orchids do not want intense sunlight, do provide some shading for them, such as shade cloth (available at suppliers in such percentages as 55, 65, 75 percent blocked) to eliminate some sunlight. Or use roll-ups, blinds, or curtains to prevent direct, intense sun rays from scorching plants. You can also build a simple lath house which will help protect orchids from direct sunlight.

Most homes lack the proper free flow of air vital for orchids—no orchid will grow in stagnant air. In the summer, you can leave your windows open, but in the winter it might be too cool outside, so run a small fan at low speed to keep air circulating. If outside temperatures drop drastically, into the 40s, move plants away from windows, yet still have air circulating. Orchids need fresh air, but not drafts.

With the problems of heating, humidity, and ventilation solved, your orchids should

flourish indoors as long as you water and feed them correctly, use the right potting mixes, protect the plants from insects or disease, repot them at the correct times, promote bloom, and shade the plants from the direct sun. Remember, your home does not have to be a jungle for you to successfully grow orchids; if the conditions are comfortable for you, they will be for your orchids, too.

None of these requirements are difficult to fulfill. For example, simply look at an orchid to know when to water it: limp leaves. And with feeding, vital for proper orchid growth, it is more a matter of knowing *when* to feed plants and how to feed them.

WATERING

If you can drink the water from your tap, it is safe for your orchids. If you live in an area with a high concentration of chlorine and fluoride in the drinking water, let the plant water stand overnight so these chemicals can dissipate.

Tepid water is better than cold water. Water in the morning so your plants will dry out by nightfall; damp plants are vulnerable to fungus disease. (If necessary, an occasional watering in the afternoon will not harm the durable orchids.) When you apply the water, be sure to *thoroughly* moisten all the fir bark (the potting medium—I'll discuss it later); this sometimes requires a great deal of water, say if the plant is newly potted. Water at the sink, or water plants in place if large saucers are underneath the pots. Let the

water flow through the pot to the saucer, empty the saucer, and repeat the process.

Small orchids dry out faster than those in large containers, and plastic pots retain moisture longer than terra-cotta pots. However, clay pots release moisture slowly through evaporation, and the increased humidity is good for orchids. Orchids grown on bark or tree fern slabs dry out very fast and need watering more often than plants in pots.

Here is my watering schedule for Cattleyas, Ascocentrums, Phalaenopses, Ascocendas, Vandas, Epidendrums, Oncidiums, and evergreen Dendrobiums:

Plants in 2- to 4-inch terra-cotta pots: four times a week in warm weather, two or three times a week in cold weather.

Plants in 4- to 7-inch clay pots: three times a week in warm weather, twice a week in cold weather.

Plants in clay pots larger than 7 inches: twice a week year-round except in the winter, then once a week.

For deciduous orchids like some Dendrobiums, I follow the following watering schedule for all plants in any size container: Severely dry out the growing medium after the orchids bloom; do not water until you see new growth starting. Then water three times a week in the spring and the summer and once or twice a week in the fall and the winter. To promote bloom, taper off watering and feeding before the seasonal bloom time.

Opposite: Lycaste aromatica

Drip System Installation

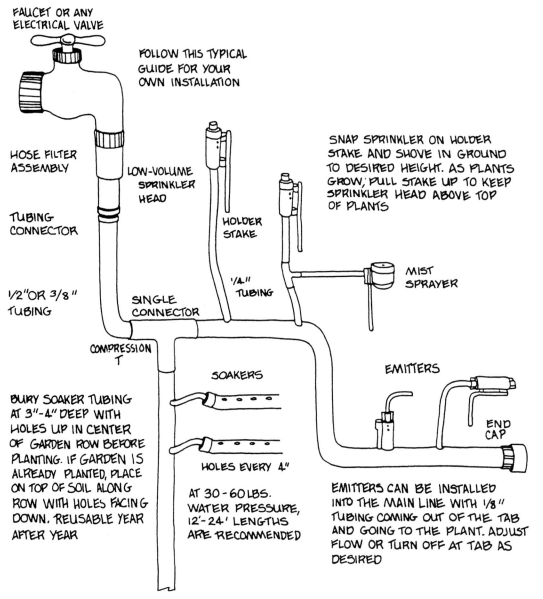

FAUCET OR ANY
ELECTRICAL VALVE

FOLLOW THIS TYPICAL
GUIDE FOR YOUR
OWN INSTALLATION

HOSE FILTER
ASSEMBLY

LOW-VOLUME
SPRINKLER
HEAD

SNAP SPRINKLER ON HOLDER
STAKE AND SHOVE IN GROUND
TO DESIRED HEIGHT. AS PLANTS
GROW, PULL STAKE UP TO KEEP
SPRINKLER HEAD ABOVE TOP
OF PLANTS

TUBING
CONNECTOR

HOLDER
STAKE

1/2" OR 3/8"
TUBING

1/4"
TUBING

MIST
SPRAYER

SINGLE
CONNECTOR

COMPRESSION
T

SOAKERS

EMITTERS

BURY SOAKER TUBING
AT 3"-4" DEEP WITH
HOLES UP IN CENTER
OF GARDEN ROW BEFORE
PLANTING. IF GARDEN IS
ALREADY PLANTED, PLACE
ON TOP OF SOIL ALONG
ROW WITH HOLES FACING
DOWN. REUSABLE YEAR
AFTER YEAR

HOLES EVERY 4"

AT 30-60 LBS.
WATER PRESSURE,
12'-24' LENGTHS
ARE RECOMMENDED

END
CAP

EMITTERS CAN BE INSTALLED
INTO THE MAIN LINE WITH 1/8"
TUBING COMING OUT OF THE TAB
AND GOING TO THE PLANT. ADJUST
FLOW OR TURN OFF AT TAB AS
DESIRED

(M. Valdez)

Drip System Watering

I have been a proponent of drip system watering from its inception and even wrote a book about it in 1979. Drip system watering involves directly applying specific amounts of water slowly and at frequent intervals directly to plants. Many of my friends who grow orchids use drip systems and have obtained very healthy plants. No water is wasted—important in drought years—and orchids receive water where they need it most, in the fir bark.

Water administered by a drip system is applied only to the plants' roots. The water comes through emitters (holes) located at selected points along water-delivery lines. The lines are small-diameter plastic tubes installed above the plants, generally on wooden rails or aluminum moldings. Some manufacturers of drip systems also offer misting emitters, which those orchids that prefer misting will thrive under. The drip system is connected to your water supply; pressure valves control the water. Necessary equipment for installing a drip system is sold at hardware stores, at garden centers, and through mail-order suppliers. You can install your own system in a few hours. The automatic timer will do most of the work for you once the system has been installed.

Misting and Humidity

Misting the foliage of certain orchids such as Phalaenopses can destroy the plants because water lodges in leaf axils and causes rot, and water sprayed directly on buds can cause buds to drop. The rain forest atmosphere the Victorians so widely advocated for orchids simply does not work. Once orchids are in cultivation, adequate moisture in the air—50 to 70 percent—is all that is required. If your home is very dry and you must mist plants, spray only the pot and potting medium to provide some temporary humidity.

One of the easiest ways to provide additional humidity for orchids indoors is to set the pots on trays of gravel. Use about 1 inch of gravel, and keep the tray filled with water to the top of the gravel. Evaporation will provide the plants with some humidity. You can also spray the growing area with a fine mist every day or so in warm weather to add some, but not a great deal of, moisture to the air. If you are growing many orchids, the plants will maintain their own humidity as they transpire through their leaves.

Although humidity is certainly an important factor in growing orchids, it is not the main consideration for success. Humidity trays (waffle-type devices to put plants on), pebble trays, and even growth trays supply the needed amounts of humidity and air movement, but I have never used them. Many plants growing together create their own level of humidity, and in the South, excess humidity is rarely needed. But if you feel you should increase the humidity for your orchids, try some of the many devices made for that purpose. You will find these items at nurseries, garden shops, home centers, and so on.

Patio Drip System

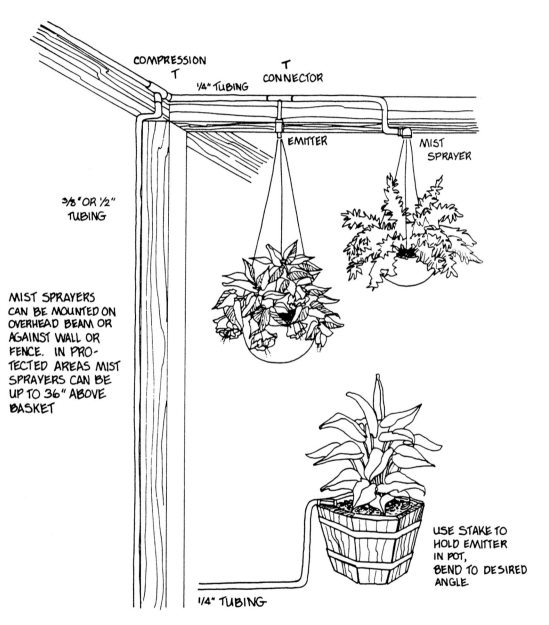

COMPRESSION T

¼" TUBING

T CONNECTOR

EMITTER

MIST SPRAYER

⅜" OR ½" TUBING

MIST SPRAYERS CAN BE MOUNTED ON OVERHEAD BEAM OR AGAINST WALL OR FENCE. IN PRO- TECTED AREAS MIST SPRAYERS CAN BE UP TO 36" ABOVE BASKET

USE STAKE TO HOLD EMITTER IN POT, BEND TO DESIRED ANGLE

¼" TUBING

(M. Valdez)

ℱEEDING

The many brands of plant foods (Spoon-it, Schultz, Peters, Oxygen Plus, etc.) come in many forms: granules, liquids, systemics with food. Plant foods consist of nitrogen, phosphorus, and potash, marked in that order by percentage on the packaging. For example, 30-20-10 means 30 percent nitrogen, 20 percent phosphorus, and 10 percent potash, with the remaining 40 percent consisting of filler (mostly other elements). Nitrogen promotes good leaf growth, phosphorus helps stems and flowers, and potash induces general vigor.

I use the Peters orchid foods, made especially for orchids. I apply the basic 30-10-10 orchid food for all-purpose feeding three times a month in warm weather, twice a month in the winter. I also use Peters Blossom Booster (10-30-20) during seasonal bloom times, which is late spring for most orchids, summer for Cattleyas. The food is in the form of granules, which you mix with water. In each pot I apply just enough of the solution to moisten the bark. Twice a year I use a mild solution of Atlas Fish Emulsion.

Time-released fertilizers do not work well for orchids. And I do not believe in foliage feeding (spraying food on foliage) because the liquid may accumulate in young growth and cause rot.

Never apply any plant food when the fir bark is totally dry. Never apply food if the sun is shining directly on the orchids. And never feed a sick orchid. Thus, follow this rule: Use plant foods on healthy orchids that have been watered and are in a light but not sunny place. Remember that it is better to feed lightly rather than heavily and to feed more when plants are growing rather than resting.

Here is my feeding program for Cattleyas, Cypripediums, Phalaenopses, Ascocendas, Vandas, Epidendrums, Oncidiums, and evergreen Dendrobiums:

Plants in 4- to 7-inch terra-cotta pots: standard plant food (30-10-10) twice a month from August to January, bloom booster (10-30-20) from February to August.

Plants in clay pots larger than 7 inches: standard plant food (30-10-10) once a month from August to January, bloom booster (10-30-20) from February to August.

It is best to feed plants shortly after they have been watered. Feed regularly and routinely—do not skip a week. Orchids receiving too much food will display leaves with brown-tipped edges, burned from too much food. Finally, never try to force an orchid to grow, because too much food can kill it.

Many new types of fertilizing solutions, preparations, and gadgets are on the market. I have tried various of these items and have not been impressed. I have not been very successful with the time-released fertilizer pellets. A specific amount of fertilizer released on schedule throughout the year (or during several months) is not beneficial for many orchids because several varieties (for example, Dendrobiums and some Cattleyas) require food while they are growing and no food at all when they are resting. And be sure to avoid the combination fertilizer–insect repellent, which can kill orchids. I have found that applying plant food by hand is the best method of feeding plants because it enables you to control the dosage, which the automatic feeding chemicals do not.

Potting Mixes and Repotting

The following directions apply generally to most types of orchids. But be sure to read about specific genera in Chapter 6 before undertaking any repotting of your orchids because certain plants demand special conditions. Some even prefer not to be repotted, so moving them out of their containers may cause serious harm.

Before the advent of steam-dried fir bark, osmunda was the accepted potting medium for orchids. Today, osmunda, a fern, is an endangered plant that is not used. Fir bark, now the universal potting medium for orchids, is quite simple to use. The bark comes in fine, medium, and coarse grades. Medium-grade fir bark usually is sold in 1/4-inch pieces (chipped bark). It is sterile, clean, easy to work with, and relatively inexpensive: A hobby-sized bag, which will pot five or six plants, costs about $3. The bark contains virtually no nutrients.

I pot Ascocentrums in fine-grade fir bark. I grow Vandas and some Ascocendas in large-grade bark because these plants need air in their root networks, and the larger-grade bark provides more air spaces. I grow all my other orchids in medium-grade bark. Some growers in Hawaii and many Southern states use chunks of charcoal (sold in pack-

ages at nurseries); others use pieces of pots (shards); still others use gravel as a potting medium for orchids.

Be sure the package of fir bark you buy *specifically* states that the material is for orchids. Fir bark is also available as a covering for walks and paths, but that material is different from orchid bark. The walkway bark pieces are large, and there are splinters and much dust.

The average life of orchid fir bark is about 18 to 24 months, after which time the bark decays and becomes pulverized. It can turn sour and stagnant and thwart root growth. Therefore, most orchids have to be repotted annually or every 2 years.

To repot, first tap the pot rim lightly on the edge of a table or countertop to loosen the root ball. Then grasp the crown of the plant with one hand, holding the pot with the other hand. Gently tease the plant from the container. Do not worry if you break off or tear a few roots when potting—the plants will not be harmed.

Once the orchid is out of its pot, gingerly tease away clinging old bark and examine the plant's roots. Cut off brown or brownish black roots. Do not cut off white roots, which indicate live tissue. Curl the white roots around the base of the plant. In a clean pot the same size or slightly larger than the used one, place shards and a layer of fresh fir bark. Put the plant into the pot and fill the pot with bark. Press down the bark occasionally with your thumbs so the plant is securely potted. The plant should stand upright in the container, not lean. Avoid loose potting.

Potting with Fir Bark

Place shards in pot.

Add bark.

Tamp down bark.

Tie, stake, and label.

(Carol Carlson)

The rule of thumb is to use a new pot 1 inch larger in diameter than the old pot, but sometimes a plant will fit into a pot of the same size. I find that orchids grown somewhat potbound (in pots slightly too small), especially Dendrobiums, bloom better than those in very large containers.

After repotting, do not water the plant immediately. Let the orchid recover from the shock for, say, a day or two; put the plant in a shady place during this convalescence. Then start watering.

CONTAINERS

Other than miniature orchids or certain species of orchids which are usually grown on slabs of tree fern (called mounts), your indoor orchids will be in containers. As mentioned, plants thrive in terra-cotta pots because the moisture from the porous walls of the pots slowly evaporates. Special orchid containers (clay) with slotted bottoms to allow air to reach the roots are now being sold and are excellent for orchids. Order them from mail-order suppliers if you are unable to find them in the nursery sections of large home-supply stores.

Slatted redwood, cedar, and teak baskets are also now sold at most suppliers. These replicas of the nineteenth-century baskets used in England are excellent for Vandas and other plants that need air at their roots. The baskets come in several sizes, from 4 inches to 15 inches square.

With slotted or slatted containers, use a potting mix of large-grade fir bark or lava rock.

Line the slatted containers with sphagnum to prevent pieces of bark from falling out.

Orchids can also thrive in plastic containers. Because plastic is nonporous, the potting medium in a plastic container remains moist longer than in a clay pot, which is an advantage in our warm Southern climate because you can then eliminate some watering. However, orchids in plastic containers, which are lightweight, can become top-heavy unless you put enough ballast (shards, gravel) in the bottom of the containers for balance. Also, suspending plastic pots on hangers from a ceiling can be a problem because usually the rim of a plastic pot will not accommodate the standard wire hanger. This is a detail worth considering because many orchids like to be suspended close to windows to receive maximum light.

Any container, clay or plastic, must be scrupulously cleaned. Before reusing any container, scrub it thoroughly with scalding water and rinse it well. Do not pot directly in decorative containers like jardinieres, cachepots, and urns. Instead, pot your orchid in a clay pot and place that pot on a saucer and put the pot and saucer inside the decorative container; the saucer will catch excess water. For a final decorative touch, add green moss (sold in hobby-sized bags) to the top of the pot to make the container and orchid look handsome. Occasionally replace the moss when you water; after some time, moss becomes water-soaked and insects might appear. We consider containers more in the following chapter, which addresses the question of where to place

Mounting on Bark

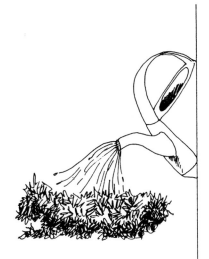

Moisten moss.

Tie in place with string.

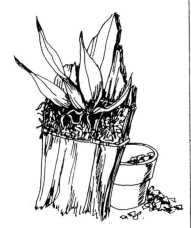

Position plant.

(Carol Carlson)

Add moss, tie again and mist.

your indoor orchids for growing and viewing.

PLANT PROTECTION

Generally, orchids grown indoors are not subject to heavy attack by insects. Because orchids are grown in bark rather than soil, you can see any insects that are present; insects and their eggs can lurk in soil but not in fir bark. And since orchid foliage is succulent and thus tough, not many insects will try to dine on the inedible greenery; most bugs prefer leafy plants.

But occasionally pests do strike. Hot weather is a favorable condition to many insects, so be on the alert for insect problems. Watch for streaked, blotchy, or eaten leaves. And do remember that sometimes even maximum care will not get rid of the pests.

Before you go into battle, know exactly what insects you are fighting. When you do find invaders, use botanically based repellents and old-fashioned remedies rather than chemicals. Do not trust the so-called safe chemicals on the market; help save the environment when fighting bugs and plant diseases.

Mealybugs are cottony pests about 1/8 inch in diameter. Aphids are oval-shaped. Scale insects are brown or blackish and oval-shaped. To kill these bugs, dip a cotton swab in rubbing alcohol and directly touch the pests with the swab. Repeated applications are necessary. Use a pesticide *only* if the infestation is severe.

Orchids are most bothered by ants, which love to hide in the bark and build nests. If ants infest your orchids, mealybugs are bound to appear because ants are great herders of mealybugs, establishing colonies of them as a source of protein for their young. If you see ants, immediately flush the potting medium with water and then use one of the several available ant repellents, such as Grant's Ant Stakes.

Slugs and snails feast on orchids if nothing else is available. Routinely douse your plants with slug and snail bait to keep them away. Corys, an excellent snail and slug bait, also controls ants.

The red spider mite occasionally attacks orchids. This pest is hard to see, but evidence of its work includes silvery leaves and streaked leaves.

Fungus disease (*botrytis*) can attack orchids if the light is insufficient and the air in the growing area contains too much moisture. Fungus infections cause mildewed, powdery, mushy growth. The best remedy is to cut away the infected parts immediately and dispose of them.

Virus disease in orchids is now less a problem than it was a few years ago because most stock used for propagation today is virus resistant. Immediately remove and burn leaves with streaked or spotted areas (concentric rings). A dependable chemical preventative for virus in orchids is still not available.

With leaf spot, brown spots appear on leaves, usually caused by too-moist conditions coupled with cloudy days. Carefully cut away the infected leaf and then dust the wound with ground-up charcoal. Keep the plant somewhat dry for the next several days.

Brown spot manifests itself as large and somewhat watery spots on foliage. Splashing water-carrying bacteria onto leaves usually

Common Insects

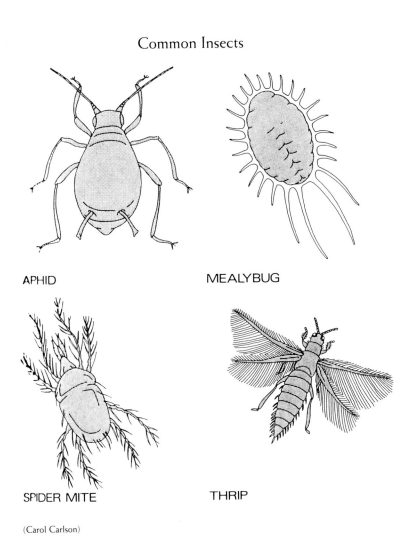

APHID

MEALYBUG

SPIDER MITE

THRIP

(Carol Carlson)

causes this malady. Cut away infected parts; dust with charcoal.

Rust appears as orange or brown raised spots, usually on the undersides of leaves. Cut away infected parts and dust with charcoal.

Anthracnose, a common disease, causes brown rings and sunken spotting on foliage. Remove diseased areas and destroy them.

Old-Fashioned Remedies

The pests most likely to attack orchids are aphids, mealybugs, scales, and red spider mites. A very old-fashioned remedy works on all these critters: a solution of $1/2$ pound of laundry soap (not detergent) mixed with 2 gallons of water. Use a standard spray bottle to spray the plants with the mixture, and then hose down the plants. Several sprayings will be necessary.

Rubbing alcohol is another excellent old-fashioned remedy. Apply it with cotton swabs directly to the pests. Repeated applications are necessary, say twice a week for 2 weeks.

"Safe" Insecticides

In the past few years, so-called safe insecticides have appeared on the market. Do not use any of these chemicals to eliminate plant insects. I have found that these insecticides cause problems for orchids. If you have an orchid that is really ailing despite your best old-fashioned remedies and vigilance, use the very effective isolation technique of separating the infected orchid from the healthy orchids. Keep the "patient" dry and out of the sun, and observe it daily to see how it is coming along. Since most orchids are tough, often an ailing orchid that is isolated and tended to will recover on its own.

Grooming

Well-groomed plants are likely to be healthy plants. Grooming consists of keeping foliage clean, removing infected foliage, removing faded flowers and trailing stems immediately, and making sure the plants are growing upright rather than leaning. Occasionally wash leaves with a damp cloth; do not use leaf-shining preparations, because they can clog pores. Use a little bit of laundry or bar soap on a cloth; flush away the soap with a spray of water.

Remove and discard all old flowers before they fall off since decayed flowers invite fungus disease. With Phalaenopses, cut the stem above another node to encourage a second flowering. Cut Cattleyas just above the pseudobulb, removing the dead sheath and flower spike.

Stake and tie Cattleyas and other bulbous orchids. Use the ring hoops made for this purpose, or make your own staking.

Propagation

Vegetative methods for increasing an orchid collection include divisions, offsets, backbulb growth, and flower-stem plantlets. Growing orchids from seed is time-consuming—you do not see results for 7 years or so—and meristemming is best left to experts. The vegetative propagation methods are the answer.

Division involves dividing a large plant of seven or eight growths (bulbs). You cut

Division

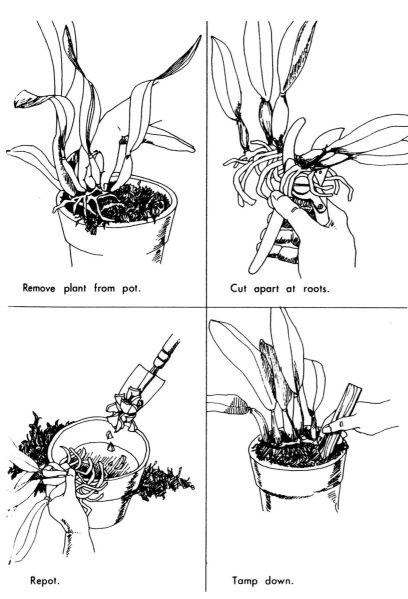

Remove plant from pot.

Cut apart at roots.

Repot.

Tamp down.

(Carol Carlson)

Offset Division

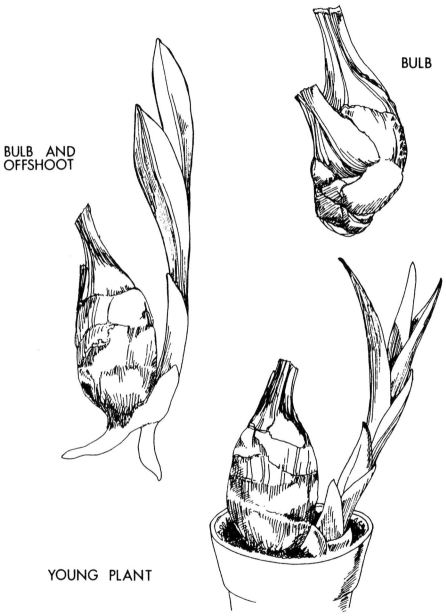

BULB

BULB AND
OFFSHOOT

YOUNG PLANT

(Bob Johnson)

off each division (bulb) and pot it. Make the cut with a sharp, sterile knife, although some-times a gentle twist will divide the plant. Cattleyas, bulbous Epidendrums, Pleuro-thalles, and Oncidiums can all be divided. Spring and summer are the best times to divide plants because orchids are actively growing then and the warm weather encourages the new plants.

After you divide a plant, put the divisions in a humid and bright location at about 70°F. Do not water the divisions for the first few days; let the plants recover from the surgical shock. Gently mist the surface of the potting medium a few times a day. After a few days, begin routine waterings.

Orchids such as the Angraecums and Phalaenopses frequently form offsets at their bases. When the offsets (keikis) have a few roots, twist them free of the mother plant or cut them off. Dip the offsets in rooting hormone and put them in a separate pot. After a few days, start watering the offsets.

Never throw away an orchid backbulb— pot it instead. Quite often a backbulb gives rise to a new plant. This method is not always successful, but it does work most of the time. Place the backbulb(s) in trays of vermiculite; apply water cautiously at first,

and then give routine humidity and warmth (78°F).

Dendrobiums and Phalaenopses often produce stem plantlets on their inflorescences. After a few roots form, remove the stem offsets and treat them as you would regular offsets.

Promoting Bloom

Getting an orchid to bloom depends on the type of plant. Usually, if plants are well cared for, watered, fed, and given sufficient light, they do bloom naturally at their seasonal times. Nonetheless, here are a few tricks I sometimes use for stubborn performers:

Dendrobiums: I dry out these plants severely if they have not bloomed on schedule. This method sometimes works.

Cattleyas: I move them to the uppermost part of the garden room, where there are warm conditions and bright light.

Oncidiums, Epidendrums: I move them about until I find a location they like; sometimes a few inches one way or another make the difference.

Phalaenopses: I decrease the evening temperature to, say, 56°F.

I do *not* increase feeding for any orchid if the plant does not bloom; too much feeding can harm many types of orchids.

The author's garden room where
orchids thrive. The structure has a roof
with skylights and is enclosed with
screen. The conditions are almost perfect
for most warm-growing specimens.

CHAPTER FIVE

Housing Indoor Orchids

The beauty of orchid flowers—whether the plants are in windows or in the greenhouse—cannot be ignored. Orchids demand attention with their attractive flowers and brilliant colors. Even a single Cattleya on a coffee table adds glamour to a setting, and the many home magazines that feature orchids as decorative accents help make orchids perhaps the most popular of houseplants.

Most orchids adapt well to indoor conditions and will grow with average home temperatures of around 80°F by day and ten or fifteen degrees less at night. In a greenhouse, you can literally grow dozens of orchids and move them into the living room or dining room when they are in bloom. There are orchids for almost every occasion and every place to bring color and beauty into your daily life.

While orchids are ideal decorative pot plants for the home, they are difficult to water if they are on a table, windowsill, or shelf because the water always finds its way to the floor or stains polished surfaces. Also, most orchids prefer bottom ventilation. To provide this ventilation, use small and attractive redwood trays (sold at nurseries) under the pots. You can also try making your own wooden trays, or you can use plastic light-fixture panels as trays—anything is good if it lets air circulate underneath the orchids.

Orchids grow best near a window in a south or east exposure. At a west window, too much heat can build up and scorch the leaves. If you do situate orchids in a west exposure, provide the shading I mentioned in the previous chapter; even a light curtain will help. In a north exposure, which receives less light than the other exposures, orchids such as the Paphiopedilums will thrive.

Most orchids, including the Cattleyas, Dendrobiums, and Laelias, need diffused sunlight. Many orchids, such as the Ascocentrums and Phalaenopses, do fine

Window Devices for Growing Orchids

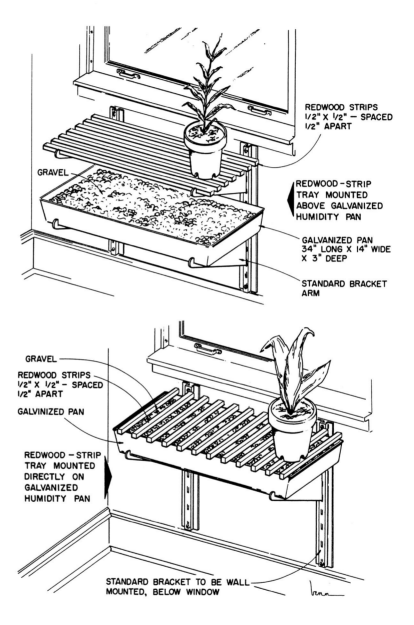

REDWOOD STRIPS
1/2" X 1/2" – SPACED
1/2" APART

GRAVEL

REDWOOD – STRIP
TRAY MOUNTED
ABOVE GALVANIZED
HUMIDITY PAN

GALVANIZED PAN
34" LONG X 14" WIDE
X 3" DEEP

STANDARD BRACKET
ARM

GRAVEL

REDWOOD STRIPS
1/2" X 1/2" – SPACED
1/2" APART

GALVINIZED PAN

REDWOOD – STRIP
TRAY MOUNTED
DIRECTLY ON
GALVANIZED
HUMIDITY PAN

STANDARD BRACKET TO BE WALL
MOUNTED, BELOW WINDOW

in filtered or diffused light but not in direct sun.

Windows

Windowsills are good spots for growing orchids, as are tables or plant stands located near windows. Be sure the tables or stands are the proper height so the plants will receive an optimum amount of light.

Growing orchids at a window requires plants of a certain height; any orchid taller than 40 inches is cumbersome and unwieldy at a window. Fortunately, most orchids now are smaller versions of their standard cousins. Art shade Cattleyas, for example, usually grow no taller than 20 inches (more about these Cattleyas in the next chapter).

If you can find them, galvanized metal planters filled with gravel and some water are good for plants; moisture evaporating from the gravel creates humidity for the orchids. Since these planters are difficult to locate, you can have some custom-made to your specifications (such as to fit a windowsill), but this is an expensive alternative. A clear acrylic tray will hold four or five plants; one or more of these trays on a table in front of a window or on a windowsill will create a handsome picture.

Glass shelves at a window always look stunning. Have a local glass house cut the glass to size, and then nail small strips of molding to the window jambs to accommodate the shelves. Even easier is a plant-shelf kit. Garden magazines advertise these kits, which include three or four glass shelves with suitable hardware for attaching the shelves to the window.

Many of the pendant orchids adapt well to growing in hanging containers, such as baskets. Any hanging container should have an attached saucer to catch excess water. If the container does not have the saucer, you must devise a drip tray on the floor.

Window Greenhouses

The window greenhouse, now very popular with plant lovers, is ideal for orchids. Kits are sold at lumberyards, home improvement centers, and even some supermarkets and generally are easy to install. You can also make your own window greenhouse from redwood, acrylic, or glass shelves. Most window greenhouses have a height restriction of about 30 inches between shelves. You can remove a shelf to make more headroom, but doing so will reduce the number of orchids you can grow.

Phalaenopsis growing in a solarium situation where it blooms yearly.

Window Greenhouse

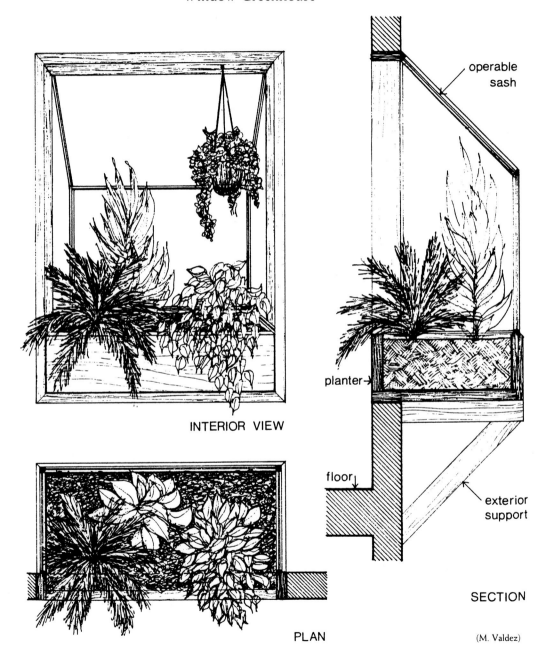

INTERIOR VIEW

PLAN

operable sash

planter

floor

exterior support

SECTION

(M. Valdez)

42

ᎶREENHOUSES

Manufactured of plastic or glass, greenhouses are available in various sizes and designs. Many greenhouse manufacturers advertise their products in the numerous garden magazines; make your selection according to your tastes and budget. To meet the conditions necessary for growing orchids, a greenhouse should be about 16 by 25 feet minimum, which is adequate for many plants (but not too many) and provides a suitably large working area.

You will find that cultivating orchids under glass or plastic is somewhat different from growing the plants in containers in rooms within your home. In a greenhouse the plants receive more light, which greatly encourages growth, but you must administer more water than you would to houseplants, watch humidity more carefully, and provide perfect ventilation. If you cannot maintain these conditions, you will be better off growing plants in containers in windows. Too much humidity and not enough ventilation can lead to orchid maladies.

An adequate heating system is vital in a greenhouse; your greenhouse and your climate will determine your needs. Ventilation and lighting are two other factors that you must also carefully consider. Greenhouses become very hot in the summer. Greenhouses should have doors for providing extra ventilation, but some manufacturers of attached structures do not provide any. Most greenhouses have built-in vents through which additional air circulates. However, make sure your unit includes *several* vents to allow

Greenhouse Furnishings

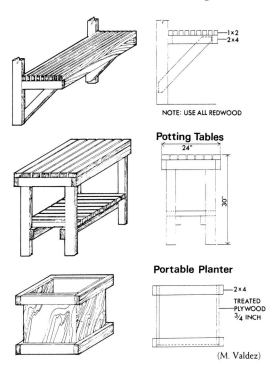

NOTE: USE ALL REDWOOD

Potting Tables
24"
30"

Portable Planter
2 x 4
TREATED PLYWOOD ¾ INCH

(M. Valdez)

enough air in. It is a good idea to install an automatic push-button ventilation system. Connect the vents to thermostats so they will open when the temperature goes above 78°F and close below 60°F. The automatic system is also a big help when you are away from home a few days, allowing you to avoid worrying about your orchids or having people come in to check on the air situation.

Most orchids will not be able to withstand hot, direct, and intense sunlight. With the exception of the Vandas and other vandaceous types, orchids like diffused light, so you must provide some type of reliable shading. The old-fashioned method of whitewashing the

These Vandas, grown close to the light in a greenhouse, show excellent care. Plants get ample light in the east-facing structure.

plastic or glass windows of a greenhouse is time-consuming but works quite well. Another effective form of shading is the shade cloth, a green plastic sheet that is strung under the glass and thus hangs over the plants. The cloth can be moved by hand to protect plants on sunny days and to let light in on days when the sun is weak. The green cloth is sold at nurseries and comes in various sizes of meshes. I prefer the cloth that lets in 30 or 40 percent of the light (check with your nursery personnel).

Adjustable overhead blinds are handsome but very expensive. Most greenhouse manufacturers sell blinds as well as inexpensive bamboo roll-ups that help thwart direct sun.

In the greenhouse, watering each pot separately with a hose is time-consuming, but it is a good way to closely observe each plant. You can tell at a glance which orchids need water and which ones do not, and the human hand is quite accurate for controlling a stream of water so that young, vulnerable growths do not rot from too much moisture.

Water in the morning, two or three times a week. As mentioned in the preceding chapter, always water early so plants will dry out by evening, eliminating any risk of fungus and mildew. I sparsely water newly potted plants until their roots can accept moisture.

Elaborate spray or misting systems are not necessary. A greenhouse has sufficient moisture because many plants are growing together. Overhead watering with a hose or misting system may cause moisture to accumulate between leaves, which can lead to rot. Also, remember that any automatic watering system will water all plants, not just those that need it, which can create havoc since many orchids rest at some time of the year.

Garden Rooms

The garden room is a glass-enclosed area, perhaps with some skylights, and it is a perfect place for growing orchids because there is enough light for plants to flourish but not so much sun that they burn. Today's garden room is a pleasant retreat from the stress and strain of everyday life. I have built many garden rooms—some quite large and a few small ones—in most of the homes I have lived in. In every case this addition was worth its weight in gold, providing a superior room for both orchids and people.

In a garden room, the same conditions prevail as in a greenhouse, except that the garden room does not become as warm in the summer, and there is no need to shade the plants from the direct summer sun. Roof 40 percent of the garden room with glass; orchids will thrive in such a situation.

Under Artificial Light

Many hobbyists grow their orchids under artificial light with considerable success, but my experience in this matter has never been entirely satisfactory because I have never invested the requisite time and patience. If you are willing to be patient and have the time to grow orchids under lights, do try this rewarding avocation.

For years, many hobbyists grew orchids under a combination of fluorescent lamps, for their blue light rays, and incandescent lamps, for the red rays. Today there are different types of light-growing lamps and bulbs, including those that combine fluorescent and incandescent light and those specifically designed for plants, such as GroLux. You can also use artificial light merely as an extra light source for your orchids.

The standard arrangement for growing plants under lights consists of lamps suspended from above and a suitable housing

The author's garden room is a screened enclosure where orchids grow on trelliswork at the rear. Orchids also are grown suspended in baskets from the ceiling.
(A. R. Addkison)

These orchids—mostly Dendrobiums—have an enviable position near windows where they receive ample bright light.
(A. R. Addkison)

for the plant containers below. When I tried growing orchids under lights, I used metal pans as trays, with 1 × 2-inch redwood slats spaced 1 inch apart placed over the trays. A standard 60-inch tray accommodates 12 to 15 plants.

Lamps for growing plants are controlled by automatic timers. I tried 15 hours of artificial light per day during the winter, 14 hours daily in the summer. I was successful with some Cattleyas, Dendrobiums, and Paphiopedilums. Other genera did not initiate buds.

You cannot grow tall orchids under artificial light because the maximum space between lamps and plants should be 48 inches, with the tops (leaves) of the orchid no closer than 2 to 3 inches from the light source. Another consideration is that orchids growing under artificial light need more watering and feeding because they are growing all the time without a rest period. This lack of rest is a problem for orchids such as Dendrobiums and Epidendrums, which like a rest period after blooming, or Lycastes, which need a rest before initiating buds.

Experimenting is necessary when using artificial light for your orchids; it takes time to find the right amount of light for the individual seasons. Aficionados of light-gardening change the light sequence by season. Thus, some orchids are short-day plants, meaning that they need long nights, while other orchids are long-day plants, requiring short nights or more light. If you are interested in growing orchids under artificial light, investigate the many new plant-growth lamps on the market. Advances in growing plants under artificial light are frequently being made; check with the mail-order suppliers listed in the many garden magazines.

Slc. Wendy's Valentine

(Hermann Pigors)

CHAPTER SIX

200 Beautiful Orchids for the South

As explained previously, selection of your orchids is a major role in whether they grow and bloom or only exist (and rarely bloom). The orchids that do well in the South are included in this chapter. The plants here are basically warm-growing or moderate-growing orchids, as opposed to the cool-growing orchids such as Odontoglossum or Coelogyne. I grew cool orchids when I lived in Chicago, Illinois, but do not cultivate them here, as creating the 55°F to 60°F nights would be difficult, and nighttime temperatures are vital to good plant growth.

The selection of plants for warm and moderate temperatures is vast. I have selected those I have personally grown, and I can vouch for their ease of culture. There are a few species more difficult to grow than others, but none are impossible to cultivate. Flowers range from small, as in Aerides, to large, as in Cattleyas, and colors cover almost every gamut of the rainbow. So, pick and choose—here are 200 beautiful orchids to grow.

Note: Sun symbol ✷ indicates orchids that will grow outside in a protected area in Zones 8, 9, 10. Bear in mind that lengthy cold spells (more than three nights) will harm the plants.

AERIDES

Aerides is a genus of epiphytic orchids native to tropical Asia. These are handsome plants in flower, and they appreciate the warmth and sun of the Southern states. The plants range in size from small to large, with leathery green leaves growing in Vanda fashion. Pendant spikes bear dozens of small but pretty flowers, usually magenta and white and sweetly scented.

As a group these are fine plants that should be grown more. Never let the temperature drop below 58°F at night, and grow the orchids in a somewhat sunny location. Aerides, although primarily houseplants, can be used in the garden when suspended from trees, where their aerial roots will attach to the trees' limbs.

Aerides lawrencianum displays multiple spikes of small white-and-purple flowers that are heavily—and wonderfully—scented. This plant, owned by the author, had over 400 flowers in one year.

Good Aerides are *A. odoratum* (probably the best one to start with), *A. japonicum*, *A. maculosum*, and *A. multiflorum*. Because these orchids do not tolerate their roots being disturbed, keep the plants 3 to 4 years before repotting. During those years, though, revitalize the pots with fresh compost at the times new growth appears.

Plants require 62 to 78°F during the day and moist conditions, at least 60 percent humidity throughout the warm summer months. In winter, decrease watering, but do not let the plants get so dry that leaves shrivel.

A. japonicum is a miniature, with 4-inch-long leaves. Its white flowers are marked red, the lip spotted purple. This Aerides is a perfect window orchid.

A. maculosum, a stout dwarf, has pale rose flowers that are spotted purple.

✿ *A. multiflorum*, a dwarf, has many small, rose-colored flowers with darker spots on the lip.

✿ *A. odoratum* is large, to 48 inches, with scapes of dozens of heavily scented, waxy, white flowers blotched magenta.

Angraecum

This genus of some 60 species is native to tropical Africa. The plants, almost all epiphytic, can grow as large as 46 inches and produce amazing flowers. The crystalline, waxy, white flowers carry long spurs, sometimes 6 inches long, giving the flowers a bizarre yet beautiful insectlike appearance. The leathery and fan-shaped leaves grow upright. Angraecums are excellent plants for shady areas because they do not want too much sun. They need water only when they are dry.

For many years *A. veitchii* and *A. eburneum* were the species grown, but newer, somewhat smaller varieties are perfect for areas where space is limited.

Grow Angraecums in medium-grade fir bark in clay pots. Do not disturb the plants until they are very overgrown in their containers. These plants resent being disturbed to the point that they may not recover from the shock of repotting for more than a year. Feed Angraecums only moderately, about twice a year; they react adversely to too much fertilizer.

A. eburneum, from Madagascar, is large (to about 4 feet), with leathery leaves. It blooms at Christmastime with 6-inch-wide, star-shaped, waxy, white flowers with long spurs.

A. philippinense is somewhat small—to about 26 inches—and in the winter produces white flowers with no spurs.

A. leonis, a great favorite, is small (to about 2 feet) and bears many very small, beautiful white flowers with short spurs.

A. veitchii is the most widely grown Angraecum. It grows about 4 feet high and bears the typical star-shaped, waxy, white flowers.

A. sesquipedale has leathery leaves and very large, waxy, white flowers.

Ascocentrum

This genus of orchids, related to the Vandas, is a small group, with only about nine species of small plants that grow to about 12 inches. These overlooked plants are easy to grow and produce lovely flowers. Ascocentrums are from warm climates, specifically China, the Philippines, Java, and Borneo. All the plants display many small flowers on each scape.

These plants like a somewhat warm location, about 80°F by day and 70°F by night. They resent cold weather, so keep them away from windows during cool nights. Water evenly, and be sure drainage is perfect because overwatering can cause problems. Most Ascocentrums bloom in spring, and the flowers emit a delightful fragrance.

☼ *A. curvifolium* grows to 28 inches, with leathery leaves. Spikes are borne between the leaves and bear many violet flowers.

☼ *A. miniatum* has narrow leathery leaves on small (10- to 12-inch) plants. There are dozens of orange blooms on short scapes. Give this plant sun.

Angraecum leonis *up close.*

(A. R. Addkison)

Left: Angraecum leonis: *This small orchid is a fine example of the genus. Plant bears numerous flowers in winter.*

(Hausermann Orchids)

Right: Ascocentrum ampullaceum

(A. R. Addkison)

ℬRASSAVOLA

This genus of epiphytic orchids is mainly from South America. Most species are small and have succulent leaves or a stemlike pseudobulb topped with one very thick leaf. The flowers are white or greenish white, quite handsome.

Brassavolas like sunlight and warmth. Pot them every year in medium-grade fir bark and allow the medium to dry out between waterings, but when you do water, flood them. The plants like a summer outdoors in heat, dappled sun, and humidity.

B. cucullata, is a small plant to 8 inches, but it bears a handsome, 3-inch, white flower.

B. digbyana, now classified as *Rhyncolaelia digbyana*, one of the larger Brassavolas, has solitary cactuslike leaves and bears a handsome, 5- to 7-inch, creamy white flower with a fringed lip. This species is frequently used for hybridization.

B. glauca, now classified as *Rhyncolaelia glauca*, seldom seen, is small, to about 14 inches, but bears lovely large, whitish green flowers.

B. nodosa, known as the Lady-of-the-Night because it is highly perfumed, has succulent, pencil-like leaves and white flowers.

ℬRASSIA

Brassia, often called the Spider Orchid, is a genus of about 40 species of unusual appearance. These epiphytic plants are native to southern Florida and Mexico, with a few from Brazil and Peru. These large evergreen plants with fantastic flowers are remarkable in that the sepals and petals are greatly elongated. *Brassia caudata*, *B. gireoudiana*, and *B. maculata* are the most popular Brassias.

These orchids have plump pseudobulbs about 2 to 6 inches long and somewhat leathery, dark green foliage 12 to 14 inches tall. The erect, or sometimes drooping, flower spikes produce numerous evenly spaced flowers that appear in the spring or summer and last 2 or 3 weeks on the plant. The fragrance of a Brassia orchid is exotic.

Brassias thrive in sun and warmth. They resent their roots being disturbed, so repot only when necessary—usually every third year—in large-grade fir bark in 8- to 10-inch clay pots. Brassias do not like too much compost around the pseudobulbs and have a

The beautiful Brassavola nodosa *growing on a piece of bark. In the evening, its flowers perfume an entire room.*

natural tendency to raise themselves out of the pot.

These plants need copious watering while in active growth; fertilizing at this time also helps (use Peters orchid food, 10-30-20). At the end of the summer, to discourage foliage growth and help initiate flower spikes, dry out the plants slightly. These epiphytes benefit greatly from additional humidity, but do not directly mist the plants, or bulb rot will result. During the winter, watering can be decreased, but do not let the pseudobulbs become dry enough to shrivel. Keep nighttime temperatures in the winter at 56 to 62°F; lower temperatures are too cold.

B. maculata produces 6 to 12 flowers, with sepals about 4 inches long and petals slightly shorter and greenish yellow spotted with brown. This is a good Brassia to start with.

B. caudata is somewhat smaller, with light green flowers sometimes tinted yellow and spotted with dark brown on the lip.

B. gireoudiana has flower scapes sometimes as tall as 24 inches and several yellow or greenish yellow flowers with a few blotches of dark brown. This is the most fragrant Brassia of the three. The species blooms irregularly with showpiece flowers.

Calanthe

This large genus of terrestrial orchids is widely distributed through Asia, China, and New Guinea, with a few from the West Indies and Central America. There are two types: large-bulb deciduous plants, such as *C. vestita* and *C. rosea,* and pseudobulbless species, such as *C. biloba, C. masuca,* and *C. veratrifolia.*

The Brassias, known as the spider orchids, bear fine flowers on graceful stems, and most exhibit this coloring.

Brassia maculata

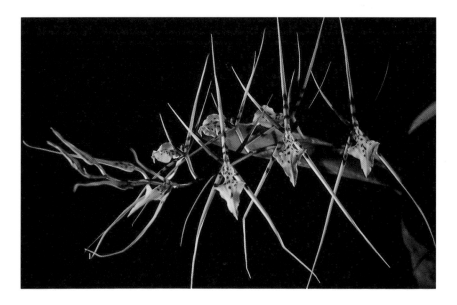

The deciduous species have elongated bulbs bearing several grassy, paper-thin leaves. When the leaves shed, the flower spike is produced from the base of the bulb and carries small white or pink flowers in late December. The plants need filtered sunlight when growth starts and full sun when leaves expand. Toward fall, when leaves shed, reduce watering. When bloom is over, store the bulbs in a brown paper sack and place in a dry, cool place. Repot in about four months.

C. vestita and its varieties are the most popular Calanthes and have 1- and 2-inch, white or pink flowers.

C. rosea produces small, pink flowers.

The evergreen Calanthes are handsome plants even out of bloom. The tall, folded leaves are dark green and grow in a compact bunch. The flowers are borne on a stout spike, many inches tall. The plants have individual rose or sometimes violet flowers about 2 inches across.

The evergreen group requires filtered sunlight, and during growth even moisture is necessary. Do not fertilize the plants, however, as this tends to burn the foliage. When new growth is completed, give the orchids a two-month rest and move to a cool place (about 50°F) with little water.

C. masuca bears many 2-inch flowers, blue-violet with pink lips.

C. biloba has stemlike growths, and the small, 1-inch flowers are purplish.

C. veratrifolia bears several 1-inch flowers; colors vary.

CATTLEYA

✷ The genus Cattleya,* with thousands of hybrids, is the best known of all the orchids and the most hybridized. Mainly epiphytes, the close to 70 species of Cattleya are widely distributed from Mexico to Brazil, although these native plants are not as large or as showy as the hybrids. When fully grown, these epiphytes have pseudobulbs 2 to 4 inches long and usually one or two stiff, fleshy leaves. Most of these plants produce flower scapes from the apex of the last-made pseudobulb; while in bud, a scape is protected by a tight sheath. Mainly summer-flowering, a great many Cattleyas are sweetly scented, and the inflorescence remains in good condition 2 to 4 weeks. Cattleyas can tolerate a wide range of temperatures, from 55°F at night to 90°F or above during the day.

The colors of the hybrids range from yellow to pink to green and almost all other colors, with contrasting lips of deep rose or red. The colors of the new meristem art shade Cattleyas are exquisite, including bright apricot petals with orange lips, orange petals with contrasting lips, and even green blossoms.

The intermarriages between Cattleya and other genera, such as Laelia, Brassavola,

*Most of the new hybrids will tolerate temperatures of 50°F at night without harm.

A typical ground orchid is this species Calanthe; originally from Africa, these orchids grow from a rhizome and most are deciduous part of the year. This variety blooms in late December.

Sophronitis, and many more, have produced plants far removed from the original Cattleya species. As a result of the hybridizing, Cattleyas are available in large, medium, small, dwarf, and miniature sizes. The large Cattleyas are about 50 inches tall; medium or art shade types grow to 20 inches; dwarfs reach 14 inches or so; and miniatures grow to about 3 inches (nonhybrid Cattleyas—those from the original species—also include true miniatures, such as *C. citrina* and *C. walkerana*). The best of the nonhybrid Cattleyas include the following:

C. amethystoglossa grows to 36 inches and bears an exquisite flower that is pale pink spotted with dark pink.

C. bicolor, a fall bloomer, displays 4-inch, green-lavender flowers that are dramatic.

C. bowringiana, an old favorite, is an erect plant that grows to 40 inches, with clusters of 3-inch, lilac-colored flowers.

C. harrisoniae is a typical pale pink flowering orchid. It is becoming scarcer but is highly desirable.

C. velutina has orange-brown flowers. The large lip is pale pink and spotted.

Dwarf species are ideal for window growing; a shelf can accommodate six or eight plants. *Cattleya aclandiae, C. citrina, C. dolosa, C. forbesii, C. nobilior, C. skinneri, C. o'brieniana,* and *C. schilleriana* are excellent dwarfs.

Growing Conditions

The extensive hybridizing and mixed parentage truly have produced flowers of better form, substance, lasting quality, and adaptation to temperature, but these are also the same factors that make knowing exactly how to grow Cattleyas difficult. Following are general specifications for average conditions.

Cattleyas like moisture in the air; 40 to 50 percent relative humidity is fine for most varieties. Air circulation is vital, including air circulating from the bottom of the pot, to allow the roots and the potting medium to dry properly.

In their native habitats, Cattleyas grow mainly in treetops under a canopy of leaves, receiving dappled or filtered sunlight, not direct sun. Provide filtered light, such as through a sheer curtain or through patterned window glass. An east exposure is fine because it provides bright morning light. Cattleyas can also thrive in the bright but somewhat warmer light from a southern exposure. Even a north window can accommodate some orchids, such as *Cattleya citrina.*

Avoid a west exposure because heat can accumulate, and the direct sunlight can burn foliage.

Watering and Feeding

Cattleyas need sufficient water, but never drench the plants. If your plants are in 5-, 6-, or 7-inch pots, water them at least twice a week (three times a week during warm weather). Larger pots need not be watered as often because they will retain moisture longer. In the winter, when the weather is cooler, water less often, but never let the plants get bone dry.

Water Cattleyas thoroughly, and let the tepid water drain through the medium. You have to water your plants at the sink to thoroughly water; scanty watering can harm

Opposite: Cattleya guttata
(Hermann Pigors)

Brassocattleya Maikai 'Mayumi', a favorite small orchid, shows beautiful form.

plants by wetting only pockets of the medium, making roots work to find moisture.

Fertilize Cattleyas with a general, all-purpose 30-10-10 formula until late summer, then switch to Peters orchid food (10-30-20) during the fall and winter. Twice a year apply a light solution of Atlas Fish Emulsion. Generally, fertilize four times a month when plants are actively growing. Use enough plant food so it runs through the bark and wets it thoroughly.

Potting Mixes and Repotting

Use a standard, medium-grade fir bark. Small pots work best for Cattleyas. In pots larger than 7 inches in diameter, the bark holds water too long, and excess water can harm plant roots. Growing Cattleyas on pieces of bark, tree fern slabs, or cork works only with smaller species, such as *C. citrina* and *C. walkeriana;* most Cattleyas are too large and awkward in growth for "mounted" potting.

Follow the potting "rules" discussed in Chapter 4. Repot Cattleyas every 12 or 18 months, no longer than 4 weeks after plants bloom. This timing is crucial: Later, too many roots may have formed and then be injured in the repotting process. Allow 1 inch between the new growth and the edge of the fresh pot so the plant will have enough room in which to grow for a year or so.

Dwarf Species

C. aclandiae produces one or two giant flowers 4 inches in diameter. The flowers are olive-green and blotched with brown-purple, the lip magenta with darker purple. Grow this dwarf on a slab of tree fern rather than in a pot.

C. citrina is one of the few of the genus that blooms in pendant fashion. The cup-shaped flowers, 2 inches across, are a very pretty bright yellow. Since this is a pendant-growing plant, grow it on a block of wood or slab of fern.

C. dolosa has magenta flowers with a yellow disk in the lip. The plant flowers in the winter.

C. forbesii carries two to five flowers that are 3 1/2 inches in diameter. The lip of the greenish yellow flower is streaked with red on its inside.

C. nobilior, most unusual, displays delicate, rose-colored flowers, the inflorescence borne on a separate leafless stem.

C. o'brieniana bears one to three large, rose-colored flowers; the front part of the lip is a darker rose.

C. schillerana offers large, dark rose-brown flowers 4 inches across; the dark rose lip is edged with pink. This orchid blooms in late summer. When the pseudobulbs mature, give the plant a 5- to 7-week bone-dry rest.

Art Shade Cattleyas

The colors of the art shade Cattleyas (also called novelty crosses) range from peach to apricot to orange to light pink and rust, with numerous shades between. The plants purposely have been bred to be small (as compared to the larger white or lavender hybrids), providing compact, easy-to-handle orchids appropriate for small rooms. Most art shades bloom twice a year, and many can adjust to varying conditions.

The parentage includes Sophronitis, Brassia, and Laelia, producing spectacular

3-to 6-inch flowers. The flowers last about 4 weeks, and there are varieties for almost every season. Grow these varieties in intermediate conditions of about 56°F minimum at night. Keep the plants shaded from the summer sun, but give them bright light in the winter. Keep the bark potting mix evenly moist at all times, and feed the plants three times a month.

Art shade hybrids: The bloom season for these amber, peach, pink, and rust hybrids is mainly autumn and winter.

Slc. Kauai Starbright 'Vi' × C. Chocolate
    Drop 'Kodama' CR/HOS, AM/AOS
Lc. Mary Ellen Carter
Bc. Lynn Gaine
Pot. Caesar's Head
Blc. Helen's Fortune
Blc. Hawaiian Holiday
Slc. Naomi Kerns 'Fireball'
Blc. Malworth 'Orchidglade' FCC/AOS ×
    Slc. George Hausermann
Lc. Chicanery × Blc. Orange Nugget
    'Kadaoka' HCC/AOS
L. Coronet × C. Mt. Shasta × Slc. Tickety Boo
Lc. Gold Digger 'Orchidglade's Mandarin'
    AM/AOS × Slc. Hazel Boyd 'Sunset'
    AM/AOS
Slc. Little Beamche × Epi. cordifolium
Slc. Little Beamche 'Richella' HCC/AOS ×
    Slc. Sunset Glow 'Richella'
Blc. Manu Flirt 'Chee' × Blc. Orange Nugget
    'Kadaoka' HCC/AOS
Slc. Orange Mist × C. Small World
Lc. Pixie Gold 'Muse' AM/AOS × Blc.
    Bouton 'D' or 'Lewis' AM/AOS

C. schilleriana × Slc. Jewel Box 'Scheherazade'
    AM/AOS
L. tenebrosa × (C. aclandiae × C. Antigo)

Yellow Cattleyas

The yellow varieties of Cattleyas are bright, charming, and blend well with almost any interior decor. Also, many of the yellow varieties have a pleasing fragrance. Some of the Cattleyas are yellow throughout (concolor); many also have the traditional and more dramatic red lip.

Species such as C. luteola, C. flava, and C. citrina have been used extensively for the intense hybridization of the yellow Cattleyas; these species impart pure yellow and small flowers. Flowers 3 inches in diameter appear on plants such as Laeliocattleya Golden Girl 'Miami' AM/AOS and Brassolaeliocattleya Arlene Finney 'Sunny.' However, a great many large, yellow varieties produce flowers up to 7 inches across, including Blc. Frank Reyes 'Dee' and Blc. Hausermann's Yellow-Wood 'Chartreuse.'

Note that not all of the countless hybrids have good flower substance. For example, some yellow Cattleyas are weak in substance compared to the green varieties. Lasting quality also varies; the flowers of plants with Pacific Gold lineage can stay beautiful on the plants for 5 or 6 weeks. However, there are many good yellow varieties available, and they can provide flowers in the fall, winter, spring, and even summer.

The yellow Cattleyas grow well with routine Cattleya culture, but they need somewhat more light than the green or red varieties. They also need more moisture and liberal feeding than the other Cattleyas.

Some excellent yellow Cattleyas cost as little as $30; others may cost as much as $100. My favorites are those with Amber Gold or Amber Glow heritage.

Yellow hybrids: These fine plants bloom in the summer, autumn, and winter. Here are my favorites.

Blc. Melinda Wheeler 'Halcyon' HCC/AOS × Blc. Golden Embers 'Chris' AM/AOS

Blc. Golden Embers 'Chris' AM/AOS × Blc. Malworth 'Orchidglade' FCC/AOS

Blc. Ethel DuPont 'Canary' × Jane Helton 'Orange Gem'

Lc. Amber Glow 'Kathleen' AM/HOS × Blc. Buttercup 'Robin'

Blc. Bouton 'D' or 'Rainbow' SM/SFOS × Blc. Buttercup 'Robin'

Slc. Rosemary Clooney 'Nanae' AM/AOS × C. aurantiaca

Slc. Tangerine Jewel x L. briegeri

Pot. Tapestry Peak 'Yellow' × Blc. Buttercup 'Robin'

Cattleya: Blc. Hausermann's Paprika 'Sunset Ridge' is a superlative cultivar. Blc. Sunset Gorge and Blc. Golden Embers are its parents.
(Hausermann Orchids)

Lc. Chine 'Bouton d'Or' × Lc. Ann Follis
Lc. S. J. Bracey 'Field' SM/SFOS × Lc.
  Edgard van Belle 'Mesbla'

Red Cattleyas

The red flowers of the Cattleya hybrids demand attention. Within the red color range are various shades and tones of true red. For example, Sophrolaeliocattleya Jewel Box 'Dark Waters' has brilliant orange markings within the lip, Slc. Mae Hawkins 'Miya' HCC/AOS is true blood red, and Slc. Naomi Kerns 'Fireball' is a rather subtle red.

Flowers can be somewhat small, as in Slc. Jewel Box 'Dark Waters,' to large, as in Potinara Rebecca Merkel 'Sangre de Paloma.' Many of the red hybrids bloom twice a year; failure to bloom can be caused by cultural problems or the habit of the particular plant itself.

The red Cattleyas of this breeding prefer some coolness; I keep my red hybrids 5 to 7 degrees cooler at night than I do my Brassiocattleyas or Laeliocattleyas. In summer, provide heavy shade for Sophrolaeliocattleya varieties with 40 percent shade cloth. The red Cattleyas follow the same watering and feeding schedules as the other Cattleyas.

The red hybrids are more floriferous than the green varieties, but the lasting quality, about 3 weeks under average conditions, does not compare to the 5 weeks or more common for green varieties. A mature, good red hybrid will cost $50 or more since the red hybrids are much more in demand than the lavender or white Cattleyas.

Red hybrids: These Cattleyas bloom in the autumn and winter. Following are some of the red hybrids I have cultivated that have proved to be excellent.

Pot. Rebecca Merkel 'Denise Trowbridge'
  AM/AOS
Slc. Jewel Box 'Dark Waters' HCC/AOS
Slc. Falcon Westonbirt FCC/RHS
Slc. Riffe 'Burlingame' AM/AOS
Pot. Rebecca Merkel 'Sangre de Paloma'
  GM/SFOS
Stc. Naomi Kerns 'Fireball' AM/HOS
Slc. Madge Fordyce 'Red Orb' AM/JOS
Slc. Tropic Dawn 'Fire Flame' AM/AOS
Slc. Mae Hawkins 'Maya' HCC/AOS
Blc. Gift 'Glory Gold'
Slc. Hazel Boyd 'Royal Scarlet' SM/JOGA,
  AM/AOS
C. Chocolate Drop × *Broughtonia sanguinea*
  'Yellow Eyes'

Green Cattleyas

The exotic green Cattleyas look dramatic in any setting. In the 1960s, Dr. Kenneth Schubert, of Clarelen Orchids in Wisconsin, produced a handsome, small, green Cattleya with a purple lip. Since then, other growers have made great strides in creating beautiful green orchids, such as Brassolaeliocattleya Ports of Paradise 'Emerald Isles' FCC/AOS. Overall, the green Cattleyas outperform the red varieties. The flowers last longer, and the plants are easy to grow with moderate care.

Many of the green varieties' heritage has some remnants of the species C. bicolor, C. guttata, and C. granulosa. Some green varieties,

such as Blc. Greenwich 'Elmhurst' AM/AOS, have rather small flowers (to 4 inches in diameter), but plants such as Blc. Pennsylvania Spring 'Orchidglade' bear large (6-inch) flowers. Most green Cattleyas sport a purple or plum-colored lip, but some varieties, such as the Emerald Isles ones, display all-green flowers.

For flower form, color, and easy culture, I favor Laeliocattleya Kencolor × Lc. Irish Helen, which is quite vigorous. I prefer the Emerald Isles varieties for lasting qualities; the blooms can last up to 5 weeks if the plants are kept in a moderate temperature. Most green varieties bloom in the fall or winter. Generally, all green Cattleyas have excellent flower substance; flowers are heavy and crisp to the touch. However, because of their popularity, these varieties are expensive: Expect to pay at least $50 for a fine, mature green orchid.

The heritage of these plants indicates a need for a somewhat humid environment, but average home temperatures of 58°F by night and 68 to 78°F by day are fine. Keep your plants evenly moist, never too wet, and maintain about 30 percent humidity. A somewhat diffused light is best for these plants. I always shade green varieties in the summer with 30 percent shade cloth.

Green hybrids: Overall, the bloom season for these desirable orchids is variable.

Blc. Envy x Blc. Verdant Venture 'Jax 2'
Lc. Ann Follis × Blc. Verdant Venture
Bc. Binosa × *Epi phoeniceum*
Lc. Ann Follis × *L. xanthina*

Blc. Greenwich 'Elmhurst' AM/AOS
Lc. Kencolor × Lc. Irish Helen
Blc. Autumn Glow 'Green Goddess' HCC
Blc. Greenwich 'Frozen Daiquiri'
Blc. Cadmium Light 'Sweet Lime' AM/AOS
Blc. Ports of Paradise 'Emerald Isles' FCC/AOS
Lc. Ann Follis 'Green Goddess'
Blc. Greenwich 'Cover Girl' AM/AOS
Blc. Jewel Higdon 'Green Goddess' HCC/AOS
Blc. Esmeralda 'Heritage' AM/AOS
Blc. Pennsylvania Spring 'Orchidglade' SM/SFOS

Lavender and Purple Cattleyas

The traditional lavender orchid, so representative of the orchid family as a whole, never goes out of fashion, as spectacular new varieties appear. For example, Brassolaeliocattleya

Opposite: Potinara Rebecca Merkle 'Sangre de Paloma': Red is always a sought-after color in orchids, and this fine hybrid is tough to beat for dynamic color.
(Hermann Pigors)

Blc. Greenwich
(Hausermann Orchids)

There are many Cattleya lavender hybrids; this one resembles one of its parents, C. bowringiana, with numerous flowers.

Bold Ruler 'Summer Magic' is a deep lavender that defies description. In fact, the color range is dazzling within this category; the dozens of lavender shades range from the old-fashioned pink to the deeper shades. Laeliocattleya Drumbeat 'Heritage' HCC/AOS was the Cattleya prom orchid of days past and is still quite popular, with enormous 8- to 10-inch flowers and a brilliant plum-colored lip. Potinara Fuchsia Fantasy 'Orchidglade' AM/AOS is one of the darker shades now available. There are more than 35 lavender and purple orchid varieties, such is the scope of color in this category.

Most of the lavender Cattleyas are somewhat large, and most have enormous flowers, which are so gaudy that some growers consider them vulgar. Many varieties are intensely fragrant, and overall, flowers last 5 to 6 weeks on the plants.

Grow the lavender Cattleyas under the same conditions as the white ones, with minimum nighttime temperatures of 60°F and as much diffused sunlight as possible.

Keep the plants evenly moist year-round, neither too wet nor too dry.

Lavender and purple hybrids: These hybrids have variable bloom seasons.

Lc. Harold Carlson × Lc. Princess Margaret × Blc. Debbie Dramm
Blc. Katherine Henby
Blc. Liese Pigors × B. digbyana
Blc. Liese Pigors × Lc. Bruno Alberts
Blc. Liese Pigors × Blc. Mem Cripsin Rosales
Bc. Marcella Koss × Lc. Irene Finney
Bc. Marcella Koss × Blc. Liese Pigors
Lc. Irene Finney × Time-Life
Lc. Island Song × Stephen Oliver Fouraker 'Elmhurst' HCC/AOS
Lc. C.J.A. Carbone × Lc. Time-Life
Lc. Stephen Oliver Fouraker 'Elmhurst' HCC/AOS × Enid Alba
Pot. Ronald Pallister 'Ron' AM/AOS × Blc. Roslyn Reisman
Blc. Dinsmore 'Perfection' FCC/AOS × Blc. Sylvia Fry 'Supreme' AM/AOS

White and Semialba Cattleyas

Along with the lavender Cattleyas, the white ones have been for years the stock in trade of cut flowers. Cattleya Bow Bells (C. Edithiae × C. Suzanne Hye), a flower of regal proportions and immense beauty, was introduced in 1945. And although there has been much hybridization since, C. Bow Bells is still regarded as a superior plant. Most white Cattleyas have large flowers (to 7 inches in diameter), many to a scape, and the throat is usually marked with golden yellow. The long-lasting and very large flowers have incredible keeping quality, some up to 6 or 7 weeks.

The semialbas are the white varieties with vibrantly colored lips, usually purple or red. The large and dramatic flowers are beautiful when displayed, as in Laeliocattleya Stephen Oliver Fouraker × Lc. Mrs. Frederick Knollys. Both the white and semialba Cattleyas are usually large plants, some to 40 inches tall, but smaller plants with smaller flowers have been introduced, such as C. Angelwalker 'Easter' AM/AOS.

Most of these Cattleyas are fragrant, some intensely so, and hybridizing has produced

Cattleya Bob Betts
(Hausermann Orchids)

white varieties for practically every bloom season. Grow the white Cattleyas at a minimum of 60°F at night and with a good deal of diffused sunlight. Give them less water than other Cattleyas, but never let them become bone dry. Keep the plants just barely moist in the winter. Feed the plants heavily during every other season.

White and semialba hybrids: These hybrids bloom in the summer, autumn, and winter.

Bc. Mount Hood 'Mary' SM/SFOS, AM/AOS
C. Angelwalker 'Easter' AM/AOS
C. Bob Betts 'Mont Millas'
C. Bob Betts 'White Lightning'
C. General Japhet 'Caracas' SM/SFOS
C. Lucille Small 'Marshall' FCC/AOS

Lc. Mount Juncal
(Hausermann Orchids)

C. Marjorie Hausermann 'York' HCC/AOS
C. Princess Bells 'Betty's Bouquet' AM/HOS
C. Swingtime 'Villa Park'
Lc. Jay Markell 'Sam Sharpe' AM/AOS-RHS
Lc. Mount Juncal
Lc. Zuiho 'Michi' AM/JOS

Splash Petal and Flare Cattleyas

The splash petal and flare Cattleyas have blotches of lavender, pink, or red against a white background. Some people love these orchids, but others find them too gaudy and very artificial looking. Most of these plants are floriferous, but the keeping quality of the flowers is poor, only about 4 weeks. The culture for the plants is the same as that for the white and lavender Cattleyas.

Hybrids that bloom in winter and spring

Blc. Buttercup × Blc. Jane Helton × Blc. Waikiki Gold
Lc. Jane Warne 'Alii' AM/HOS × C. *intermedia* var. *aquinii*
Blc. Waikiki Gold × Blc. Malworth 'Orchidglade' FCC/AOS
Lc. Ecstasy 'Orchidglade' × Lc. Gay Feather 'Catamaran'

Hybrids that bloom in autumn and winter

Lc. Chiou-Jye Chen 'Kitten Face'
Lc. Hong-Sie Chen 'Kaohsiung Beauty'
Lc. Judy Small 'Delight' AM/AOS
C. Margaret Degenhardt 'Saturn'
Lc. Olga 'Chelsea' AM/RHS-AOS
Lc. Red Empress 'Wycliffe'

Blc. Don de Michaels 'Razzmatazz'
Lc. Aqui-Finn 'Villa Park'
Lc. Aqui-Finn 'Prism Magic'
Slc. Empress of Mercury 'Gwo-Luen'
   AM/AOS
Blc. Aqui-Finn 'Splish Splash'
Blc. Gould's Glow 'Halcyon' AM/AOS
Blc. Beacon Mt. 'Gaiety' AM/AOS

Cattleytonias (Broughtonia × Cattleya):
The bloom season is variable, but usually
autumn through spring.

Ctna. Keith Roth 'Stephen Fouraker'
Bwna. Nora 'Waiomao'
Blc. Francis Hoshino × Ctna. Keith Roth
Slc. Naomi Kerns 'Fireball' AM/AOS × Ctna.
   Keith Roth
C. Chocolate Drop 'Kodama' AM/AOS,
   CR/HOS × Ctna. Keith Roth 'Richella'
Otaara Maile's Surprise
Lc. Wailea × *Broughtonia sanguinea* 'Stephen
   Fouraker'
Lc. Tropic Glow × Ctna. Keith Roth
Ctna. Sugar Plum
Ctna. Keith Roth 'Stephen Fouraker' × *Epi.
   cinnabarinum*
Blc. Oconee 'Mendenhall' AM/AOS × Ctna.
   Keith Roth 'Kodama'
Blc. Waikiki Gold × *Broughtonia sanguinea* 'Alba'
Ctna. Keith Roth 'Stephen Fouraker' (subva-
   riety Robsan) × *Sophronitis cernua*

Best of the Cattleyas

Pot. Rebecca Merkel 'Sangre de Paloma'—
   large, red flowers
Slc. Naomi Kerns 'Fireball' AM/AOS—brilliant red-orange flowers

Slc. Jewel Box 'Dark Waters'—fiery red flowers
Blc. Acapana 'Miles' HCC/AOS—large, yel-
   low flowers with orange lip
Lc. Hausermann's Summer Spectacular—
   brilliant cerise blooms with purple lip
Lc. Aqui-Finn 'Prism Magic'—white and
   pink splash petal
Slc. Orient Amber 'Orchidglade'
   AM/8WOC—orange flowers with ruffled
   red lip
Slc. George Hausermann 'Carol'
   HCC/AOS—large, orange flowers with
   red lip

CYPRIPEDIUM

Sometimes called Paphiopedilum, other
times Cypripedium, this genus of fifty
species has Asiatic origins. While the species
are seldom grown, the hundreds of hybrids

*This is a classic species
Paphiopedilum (Cypridpedium),
somewhat lesser in form and
beauty than the hybrids.*
(William Shaban)

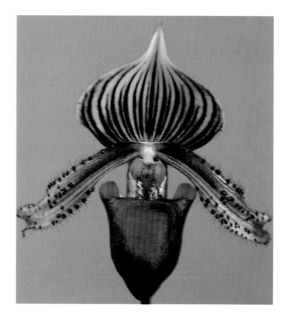

Cypripedium
(Paphiopedilum)
fairrieanum
(Hermann Pigors)

are common in collections. The flowers, borne on erect stems, are luridly colored, and the waxy inflorescence often seems more artificial than real. Most of the "Cyps" are terrestrial and need a medium of equal parts soil and fine fir bark.

These plants have never done too well for me, objecting to too much heat and humidity, but I have managed to coax a bloom or two from a few species.

The genus is without pseudobulbs and has dark green or mottled, straplike foliage. The flower spike comes from the center of the leaves and bears one or several flowers. Cypripediums dislike sun; grow them only in semishade.

C. bellatum has cup-shaped flowers, white or pale yellow and marked with purple spots.

C. insigne has brown-veined, green flowers of a shiny, waxy texture.

C. fairrieanum is an orchid that bears a multicolored flower, usually purple striped.

C. macranthum, recently introduced, produces a 2-inch flower, with typical pouch-like, pink or multicolored lips.

DENDROBIUM

Dendrobium includes more than 1,500 species widely distributed throughout the world, including India, Burma, Sri Lanka, China, Japan, Australia, and the Philippines. Because the species vary greatly in shape and habit, successful culture was difficult for the early growers. The Dendrobiums are classified into five groups: those with (1) pronounced pseudobulbs; (2) evergreen cane-type pseudobulbs; (3) deciduous cane-type pseudobulbs; and those that are (4) evergreen cane-type Phalaenopsis hybrids; and (5) black-haired, short-stemmed plants.

Group 1

These orchids have pronounced pseudo-bulbs and need a period of drying out (grow with scant watering) to encourage bloom. Generally, the less attention you give these orchids, the better they grow. Overwatering or overfeeding will quickly kill the plants. Rather than feeding, repot plants in new fir bark every second year. Provide plenty of good air circulation for this group.

Dendrobium chrysotoxum and *D. aggregatum* are easy to grow and highly recommended for beginners. These plants need 4 hours of sun daily and abundant watering until growth is mature. Then, to encourage flower spikes, give the plants a 3- to 4-week rest period without water. After the plants flower, let them completely rest without water 5 to 7 weeks. Every second year repot these plants into 4- or 5-inch pots.

✢ *D. chrysotoxum* grows 20 inches high and produces drooping, apical spikes of many 2-inch, golden-yellow flowers in the spring. This orchid often blooms from old as well as new bulbs.

✢ *D. aggregatum*, a dwarf about 10 inches high, produces from the sides of the pseudobulbs pendant spikes covered with small, scented, vivid yellow flowers. This species flowers regularly in the spring.

Group 2

The evergreen-type Dendrobiums are some-what large, growing to 48 to 60 inches, and

Cypripedium (Paphiopedilum) fair-rieanum *'Vinter's Treasure'*

(Hermann Pigors)

have leaves all year. The plants bear dramatic flowers on long stems and, while the flowers do not last too long (about ten days), ever-green Dendrobiums in bloom are a stunning sight.

The evergreen cane-type plants include *D. densiflorum*, *D. thyrsiflorum*, and *D. dal-housieanum*. Others are available but, because they are usually big plants, sometimes over 6 feet tall, they are rarely grown.

The apical leaves are broad and fleshy. Flowers are produced in pendant trusses from the nodes at the tops of the canes. They are set close together and perfectly arranged like a bunch of grapes, unbeliev-ably pretty. These orchids need dappled

Dendrobium moschatum, *quite rare in cultivation, peers at you with eyelike markings on its large flowers. This plant was purchased in 1970.*

Dendrobium chrysotoxum
(A. R. Addkison)

Dendrobium fimbriatum
(A. R. Addkison)

sunlight and even moisture throughout the year, except just after flowering, when water can be somewhat reduced for about a month.

Repot these Dendrobiums, which like warmth, every second year in fir bark into 4- or 5-inch pots. Maintain nighttime winter temperatures of 58 to 64°F, with 72 to 80°F during the day. If you have trouble getting these orchids to flower, try resting them for about 3 weeks after growth has matured. Then move them into strong light in winter, where the 5- to 6-degree drop in temperature may induce bud formation. These plants produce their beautiful flowers in the spring or early summer.

D. *dalhousieanum* has tawny yellow, almost beige, flowers faintly shaded crimson; they are 5 inches in diameter.

D. *thyrsiflorum* has bunches of striking, crystal-white flowers with an orange lip. This magnificent species should be in every indoor collection.

D. *densiflorum* is similar to the other Dendrobiums in Group 2, but its flowers are of a somewhat deeper yellow.

Group 3

The deciduous cane-type Dendrobiums, commonly called the "nobiles," produce flowers in twos and threes from the nodes along the tops of the bare canes. Species

includes *D. fimbriatum, D. nobile, D. pierardii, D. wardianum,* and *D. superbum.* The flowers are large and delicate, in shades of pink, lavender, and orange. A great many of the flowers are delightfully scented.

In growth throughout the summer, these fine orchids need moisture and warmth; suspending them in pots from tree branches is fine. When foliage has fully expanded, with a solitary leaf instead of pairs of leaves, stop watering. At this time, usually October, move the plants into cool temperatures if possible (48 to 55°F at night). Throughout the winter while the leaves fall, the plants should receive no water. When buds start showing in swellings along the nodes, move the plants back to where the nighttime temperature is 58 to 64°F. Resume waterings as buds increase in size. Repot plants every second year into 4- or 5-inch pots.

D. fimbriatum sheds its foliage every second year. This pretty, little plant bears brilliant orange flowers.

D. nobile, the most popular nobile, has white flowers tipped rose-purple, with a dark crimson blotch in the throat. This species has many wonderful hybrids; color varies.

D pierardii produces 2-inch, paper-thin, blush-white or pink flowers veined rose-purple. It is very dependable.

D. wardianum, with 2-foot stems, has white flowers tipped purple with a yellow-stained lip. This plant does not always flower every year.

D. superbum produces myriads of handsome and large lilac-colored flowers from bare silver-hued canes. This extremely attractive species needs vertical growing space because the canes sometimes grow 5 to 6 feet tall.

A true species and a stunning one, Dendrobium superbum *blooms on bare stems in spring with hundreds of flowers.*

White nobiles: These orchids bloom in the winter and spring.

Den. Hoshimusume 'Canary'—cream-colored petals and sepals, with a wide, dark-orange lip

Den. Hoshimusume 'Haming'—creamy white flowers with petals and sepals tipped light pink

Den. White Pony 'Akamatu' AM/AOS—very large white flowers

Den. Yukidaruma 'King' AM/AOS-JOS—snow-white flowers with a white throat

Dendrobium superbum alba: *This is the white form of* D. superbum. *It presents an elegant array of crystal white, graceful flowers.*

Den. Yuzuki 'Royal' CCM/AOS—large, creamy white flowers with a golden throat

Splash petal nobiles: Here are the winter- and spring-blooming splash petals.

Den. Christmas Chime 'Asuka' AM/AOS—milky white flowers with purple tips, purplish brown in the throat amid deep yellow

Den. Gion 'Pink Lady' HCC/AOS—light-colored flowers bordered with pink-purple; creamy yellow throat

Den. Happy Bride 'Orient'—creamy white flowers that are reddish purple on one-third of the petals

Den. Hoshimusume 'Smile'—creamy white flowers with hint of pink on tips; dark orange lip

Den. Momozono 'Princess'—flowers have a clear white center, reddish purple borders on the petals and sepals

Red to lavender nobiles: These nobiles bloom in the winter and spring.

Den. Andemos 'Mountain View' AM/AOS—extra-large, dark purple flowers with creamy white center

Den. Malones AM/AJOS—large, beautifully shaped, purple flowers, with dark purple throat bordered by dark yellow

Den. Malones 'Picola'—dark reddish purple flowers, with dark orange throat and small reddish brown eyes in the lip

Den. Malones 'Saitomi'—light reddish purple flowers with reddish brown throat

Den. Olympia 'Red King'—very large, thick-textured, reddish purple flowers

Den. Satellite 'Perfection'—bright deep reddish purple flowers with dark orange throat

Den. Utopia 'Luster'—flowers have large, extra-dark reddish violet sepals and petals; dark throat

Den. Utopia 'Messenger' FCC/9WOC, AM/AOS—striking dark-reddish purple flowers with dark yellow lip

Yellow nobiles: These nobiles bloom in the winter and spring.

Den. Golden Blossom 'Kogane' AM/AOS— delicate yellow flowers with a dark yellow lip

Den. Golden Blossom 'Lemon Heart'— breathtaking bright yellow flowers, golden yellow throat

Den. Golden Blossom 'Melody'—orange-yellow petals and sepals, small purple disk on the lip

Den. Golden Blossom 'Sunset' AM/AOS—the best of the yellows

Den. Golden Blossom 'Sweetheart'— canary yellow flowers with a beautiful yellow lip

Den. Golden Talisman 'Yamabuki' HCC/AOS—exquisite dark golden yellow flowers with a reddish throat

Den. Hambuhren Gold 'Eve'—yellow flowers with a greenish orange throat

Den. Pittero Gold 'Grace'—outstanding orange-yellow flowers with an orange-yellow lip

(All Dendrobium nobile hybrids are by Dr. Jiro Yamamoto.)

Group 4

The evergreen cane-type *D. phalaenopsis* grows to about 2 feet and produces flowers on short stems from the top of the cane. *Dendrobium veratrifolium,* the Antelope Orchid, is a rare species in this group. Temperatures of 72 to 80°F, with at least 4 hours of sun a day and abundant moisture, are necessary for good flower production. Never let the temperature drop below 70°F at night in the winter.

Dendrobium phalaenopsis

(A. R. Addkison)

D. phalaenopsis produces many flowers about 3 inches across; the blooms are deep rose-shaded magenta. There are many hybrids, so colors vary considerably.

D. veratrifolium produces lovely and fragrant flowers about 3 inches in diameter.

Phalaenopsis-type hybrids: These plants bloom mainly during the summer.

Den. Alice Queen—yellow-green flowers

Den. Betty Ho 'Sakata'—canary yellow flowers, red-purple lip

Den. Circe 'Gail' AM/AOS-HOS-SMOS—outstanding 4-inch, royal purple flowers; blooms year-round

Den. Esther Zane Shigaki 'Butterfly' AM/AOS—long-lasting, yellow flowers contrasted by deep red lip

A group of hybrid Dendrobium phalaenopses. These plants keep bearing flower spikes throughout the warm months. The flowers last for weeks.

Den. Floy Day 'Susan' AM/AOS—chartreuse flowers with a reddish brown lip

Den. Garnet Beauty 'Suzuki'—very large, burgundy flowers

Den. Hickam Deb 'Walcrest' AM/AOS—large, full, round, reddish purple flowers

Den. Jacqueline Concert—vigorous grower, bearing long, arching sprays of deep red-purple flowers

Den. Lim Then Hin 'Waipahu' AM/AOS—reddish purple flowers

Den. Walter Oumae—sprays of white, everblooming flowers

Group 5

The flowers of Groups 1 to 4 last 3 to 4 weeks, but those of these short-stemmed Dendrobiums last 8 to 11 weeks. *Dendrobium dearei, D. formosum,* and *D. jamesianum* are excellent species. Characterized by black-haired, silvery stems, these plants produce white flowers whose lip is usually spotted yellow or red; *D. jamesianum*, sometimes called *D. infundibulum* var. *jamesianum*, is a good one. Most species flower in late summer. The plants can be summered outdoors in direct sun once full growth is well under way. Mealybugs may attack the deciduous group; inspect your plants regularly and treat appropriately (see Chapter 4).

EPIDENDRUM (ENCYCLIA)

Epidendrum is one of the larger orchid genera, with about 1,000 species distributed mainly throughout Central America, Mexico, Brazil, and the southern parts of the United States. These were the first orchids brought into England, about 1725. Terrestrial or epiphytic, Epidendrums are variable in form: with globose, hard, egg-shaped pseudobulbs; with stemlike pseudobulbs; or without pseu-dobulbs and with flexible or reedlike stems. Flowers come in every color imaginable, and many species bloom year-round. These are ideal plants for Southern climates, either indoors or in the landscape.

Epidendrum atropurpureum (*E. cordigera*), *E. aromaticum*, and *E. vitellinum* are in the hard-bulb group, generally classed as Encyclias. Their pseudobulbs are tipped with two leaves; the arching spike from the top of the bulb bears many flowers, which last 3 to 5 weeks. These species need direct sun and tight potting in fir bark. Give the plants plenty of water while they are in active growth and until they flower. Once they begin flowering, these plants need a 3- to 5-week rest, with very little water.

E. aromaticum, about 12 inches tall, produces sweetly scented, greenish white flowers. *E. atropurpureum*, similar in habit, has brown-and-pink flowers with a red-striped lip. Both species bloom in the early spring and are amenable to home nighttime temperatures of 58 to 64°F, and 70 to 78°F during the day.

E. vitellinum is a dwarf, about 8 inches tall, with brilliant, small, red flowers. Place this charming window plant close to the glass because it likes coolness, about 54 to 60°F at night.

E. mariae, *E. nemorale*, *E. polybulbon*, ✿ *E. prismatocarpum*, *E. radiatum*, *E. stamfordianum*, and *E. tampense* represent the stemlike pseudobulb species, now classified as Encyclias. These slow-growing plants become large. They need filtered sunshine and do better when potted slightly loose in fir bark mixed with

This green-form Epidendrum hybrid is ideal for mild climates. Use in the landscape.

sphagnum moss. Supply even moisture year-round, with a slight rest for a few weeks after the plants flower. These Epidendrums are slow to come back with new growth, so do not try to force them. Average home temperatures around 70°F suit them.

✿ *E. mariae* grows to 14 inches and produces clusters of green-petaled, white-lipped flowers.

E. nemorale bears many 2-inch blush pink flowers in the winter.

E. polybulbon grows to 10 inches and displays brown flowers that last for weeks. It is easy to grow mounted on a slab of fir bark.

E. fragrans has bright yellow flowers striped vivid purple. In bloom it is really eye-catching.

✿ *E. stamfordianum* produces erect scapes of brilliant yellow flowers spotted red. The inflorescence is bunched at the top of the stem, lasts well, and is delightfully fragrant. This species produces its flower spike from near the base of the pseudobulb and prefers a complete 5- to 7-week rest (no water) after it flowers.

✿ *E. tampense* bears dozens of brown-and-green flowers that last for weeks.

The reed-stem Epidendrums without pseudobulbs are known for their constant blossoming in our southern landscapes. I have had *E. o'brienianum* in flower for more than a year in the south end of my garden; *E. elegans*, *E. nocturnum*, and *E. radiatum* are also worthwhile. These orchids need plenty of water year-round and a few hours of south or west sun daily. Repot the plants every year.

✿ *E. o'brienianum* has 1-inch flowers clustered at the top. As the lowest flowers fade,

new ones appear at the top. The species includes many varieties, and colors range from pink to lavender to brick red. In climates mild year-round, this plant will thrive outdoors in a garden (use a standard terrestrial compost).

E. nocturnum has 4-inch, greenish white flowers that are especially fragrant at night. It likes slightly cool conditions.

✿ *E. radiatum* blooms in the summer with many green flowers lined white.

GALEANDRA

Galeandras come from Central America. Only occasionally have I seen these orchids in collections, but I mention them because the one species I have grown, *G. devoniana*, is a spectacular yet easy-to-grow, warmth-loving plant. The very colorful, 3-inch flowers

A small orchid, Epidendrum fragrans bears small, waxy flowers lined purple in bunches. An elegant species.

Epidendrum nemorale: *Count on the Epidendrums for spray-type blooming. Here the flowers are small, but there are many of them.*

(A. R. Addkison)

Opposite: One of the many Epidendrums. Here you can see the detail of the flowers.

(Hermann Pigors)

Epidendrum tampense,
*an almost everblooming species
with small but pretty flowers,
likes warmth and humidity.
Plants grow easily and bloom
in the summer.*
(A. R. Addkison)

Laelia perrennii *is an
original species with somewhat
smaller flowers than the hybrid
Laelias, yet quite attractive.*
(Steve Christofferson)

Opposite: Galeandra devoniana *is a Central American
orchid with lovely large flowers
about 4 inches across. The
sepals and petals are narrow
and the lip is trumpet shaped.*
(Joyce R. Wilson)

are borne on tall, wiry stems, and the foliage is grassy and reedlike.

Grow Galeandras in small-grade fir bark in a sunny location. Water the plants frequently, especially during the fall. Flowers generally appear in the winter or early spring. Do not cut off the flower stem, because sometimes the plant blooms again on the old stem.

G. devoniana grows to 4 feet. The flowers have narrow sepals and petals, brownish purple marked with yellow. The lip is white and lined with purple.

ℒAELIA

Laelia is a genus often overlooked, but it can rival Cattleya in beauty. Only recently has extensive hybridization of this genus begun. The Laelias are allied with the Cattleyas, with about 70 species from South America. Most Laelias need a south exposure; plants bloom profusely. These sun-loving epiphytes are ideal for our warm southern climates. *Laelia anceps, L. autumnalis, L. flava, L gouldiana, L. harpophylla, L. pumila,* and *L. superbiens* are good species.

Generally, these orchids carry one or two fleshy evergreen leaves. The pseudobulbs vary in size and shape, and the flower spike is produced from the top of the pseudobulb. Several species are dwarf plants that produce brilliant yellow or orange flowers at various times of the year; others are extremely large plants, carrying spikes 6 feet long and crowded with spectacular blooms. To accommodate the large Laelias in your home, place the containers on inverted pots on the floor. Grow Laelias in front of a window or near

French doors, where they can receive ample sunlight.

The Laelias grow under such varied conditions that it is not possible to present definite culture information. Overall, the plants like plenty of sun and abundant moisture until they bloom. Winter nighttime temperatures of 52 to 56°F seem fine. Let the plants rest for 4 weeks in the winter, and then water sparingly throughout the remaining winter months. In early spring, grow your Laelias outside where they can get the sun they need (about 5 hours a day). Repot the large Laelias every 2 years in large-grade fir bark, the small ones in small-grade fir bark.

✿ *L. anceps,* perhaps the favorite in the genus, has single stems bearing 4-inch, lavender flowers.

L. autumnalis grows to about 12 inches and produces an inflorescence 4 inches in diameter,

rose or pinkish purple, with the lip white with a yellow ridge.

L. flava is small, with clusters of canary yellow flowers.

✿ *L. gouldiana* is small, to 16 inches, and has leathery leaves with a long flower spike bearing 3-inch, lavender flowers.

L. harpophylla bears dramatic orange flowers in the winter.

L. pumila, a 6-inch dwarf, has pretty, rose-purple flowers 2 inches in diameter. Here is a good Laelia to start with.

L. superbiens is a giant, 3 to 4 feet tall, with flower scapes 4 to 6 feet long. This orchid species is perhaps one of the most beautiful grown, with large clusters of 10 to 15 brilliant rose-colored flowers streaked with crimson or purple.

Laelia purpurata hybrids: These plants bloom in the summer and autumn.

L. purpurata 'Cindarisa'—6-inch, yellow flowers with a red lip

L. purpurata 'Maria Bonita'—6-inch, white flowers with a purple lip

L. purpurata 'Pedrevia'—4-inch flowers mainly white, with burgundy marking on the lip

Laelia gouldiana, *with its large four- to five-inch flowers, has been a favorite for many decades. It always blooms in autumn.*

Laelia purpurata

L. purpurata 'Doraci'—exquisite large, white flowers veined purple, with a purple lip

ℒYCASTE

With about 35 different species distributed throughout the higher altitudes of the mountains of Central America, these handsome orchids have one fault: Generally, they are deciduous. The leaves are large and thin, and many flowers are borne on single stems at the base of the pseudobulbs. The predominant flower color is yellow, but the large flower of *L. skinneri* is a blush pink.

Grow Lycastes in some sunlight, and follow a rigid watering schedule: 6 or 7 months with plenty of moisture, with a drying-out period. Grow the plants in fir bark, and fertilize them only occasionally, because they do not react well to feeding. Repot Lycastes yearly into fresh fir bark. Few Lycastes have been hybridized.

L. aromatica, known as the Cinnamon Orchid because of its aroma, grows to about 16 inches and produces small, yellow flowers.

L. cruenta, to 16 inches, also bears small, yellow flowers.

L. skinneri has large (4-inch), blush pink flowers. This endangered species is outstanding.

Lycaste macrophylla is typical of the Lycaste form, but the color is beige, unlike the usual yellow.

Talk about floriferousnous, this Lycaste aromatica takes the prize. The flowers are cinnamon scented.

Oncidium sphacelatum can bear a hundred small flowers to a mature plant. Has grassy foliage.

(William Shaban)

Oncidium

Oncidium is a large and varied genus of more than 700 epiphytic orchids distributed throughout Central America, Mexico, the West Indies, and parts of Brazil. Generally called spray orchids, most Oncidiums produce long spikes of beautiful yellow flowers marked with brown. They are welcome additions to any interior or landscape. *Oncidium ampliatum, O. leucochilum, O. ornithorynchum, O. sarcodes, O. splendidum,* and *O. wentworthianum* are good species to grow; the latter three species are excellent for window culture because they do not require as much direct sun as most plants in the genus.

Most species tolerate nighttime temperatures of 55°F. However, this family is so diversified that there are plants for many temperature ranges. *Oncidium kramerianum* and *O. papilo* do well at 72 to 80°F; *O. cavendishianum* and *O. varicosum* need 52 to 60°F; *O. crispum* and *O. splendidum* thrive at 60 to 72°F.

Many plants in this genus have compressed pseudobulbs tipped by one or two fleshy leaves, others are almost without pseudobulbs, and still others have pencil-like leaves. All Oncidiums are evergreen. The flower spike is generally produced from the base of the pseudobulb and in most cases is flexible and arching, sometimes 3 to 5 feet long. Flowers are small and numerous or large and few, depending on the species. A great many bloom in the autumn or winter, and the flowers last a long time on the plant, often 7 to 9 weeks.

Most Oncidiums need full sun for good flower production. Repot the plants every

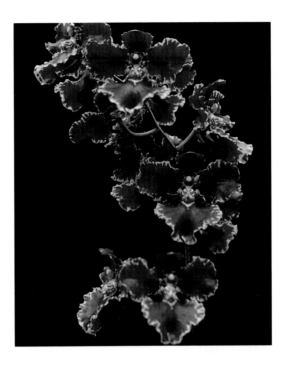

Oncidium forbesii
(Hermann Pigors)

Oncidium papilio

second year into well-drained containers of fir bark mixed with chopped tree fern. Since the plants love the sun, they require summering outside.

While in active growth, Oncidiums require plenty of water and, in most cases, high humidity (50 to 70 percent). After their flowers fade, most members in this genus need another rest period of a few weeks.

O. ampliatum has small, yellow and red-brown flowers. When flowers fade, if the same spike is cut below the last node, the plant sometimes produces a second scape.

✿ *O. leucochilum* bears yellow-green flowers barred with brown.

O. macranthum has sprays of yellow flowers on wiry spikes.

O. ornithorhynchum grows about 14 inches tall and has hundreds of tiny, lilac-colored flowers. It needs semishade and cool nighttime temperatures of 52 to 58°F in the winter.

✿ *O. sarcodes* is compact, 16 inches tall, and produces pretty, scalloped, yellow and chestnut-brown flowers.

✿ *O. splendidum*, the most commonly grown Oncidium, has solitary, cactuslike

Oncidium Gold Coin Butte: Most Oncidiums have small flowers and this hybrid is no exception, but it bears many flowers to a plant.

leaves 12 inches long, vibrant yellow flowers barred with brown, and a large and broad yellow lip.

✿ *O. wentworthianum* bears flowers about 1 inch in diameter; the flowers are a nice yellow blotched with brown.

Equitant Oncidiums: These dwarf Oncidiums have a few leathery leaves but exquisite flowers. The plants are so unusual because of the flowers' brilliant colors, and they are easy to grow if given ample sun and heat. Water these orchids year-round. They grow best mounted on small tree branches or tree fern slabs.

O. Barbie 'Strawberry Delight' blooms with tiny, brilliant red-orange flowers in the winter.

O. Golden Sunset has yellow and brown flowers in the winter.

O. Missy 'Richella' bears small yellow-red flowers.

O. Seka 'Hot Stuff' has vibrant yellow-brown flowers with red spots in the winter.

✿ *Oncidium hybrids:* Here are my favorite hybrids.

Lenalena 'Vashon' × Honolulu—medium-sized, gold flowers with dark mahogany sepals and petals flecked with gold

Waiomao Gold × Ella 'Flambeau'—yellow and brown petals and sepals; a yellow lip

Copper Falls—mahogany brown flowers with a yellow lip

Lenalena 'Vashon' × O. *sphacelatum*— purple-red flowers with white tips on petals and sepals; a whitish lip

The equitant Oncidiums have recently become available in an array of bright colors. Flowers have the standard Oncidium shape, but are small and numerous. Plants are dwarf, growing only to about 4 inches.

(Hermann Pigors)

Kutoo #1 × O. *sarcodes* #1—chocolate and mahogany-red flowers with yellow markings

Kutoo × Gold Coin Butte 'Sunshine'— golden yellow flowers with splotches of amber-brown

Maui Gold 'July'—chocolate brown petals and sepals with a fine yellow line on the edges

Kutoo × O. *sphacelatum*—chestnut brown to mahogany flowers barred yellow; yellow and red-brown-toned lips

𝒫HALAENOPSIS

Phalaenopsis, a genus of about 70 species of beautiful orchids from Java, Sumatra, the Philippines, and the Asian mainland is commonly known as the Dogwood Orchid or the Moth Orchid. These have become favorite indoor plants because they keep their flowers for months. The white flowers of the hybrids are popular for cutting. *P. amabilis, P. buyssoniana, P. esmeralda, P. lueddemanniana, P. mannii, P. rosea,* and *P. parishii* are especially fine species in this family.

The genus is characterized by the absence of pseudobulbs, and by short stems bearing three or more leathery leaves. Roots are mostly flat, often more than 2 feet long, winding in and around the pot and reaching into the air for moisture. Flower spikes are produced from leaf axils and are single or branched, short or extremely long.

Phalaenopses thrive in a warm, shady place, with 50 to 70 percent humidity. Repot these epiphytes yearly in large-grade fir bark, and try to maintain perfect drainage. Never let the potting medium become dry, and regularly apply liquid fertilizer to promote healthy growth. Never let the nighttime temperature drop below 54°F. After blossoming stops and flowers fade, snip off the stem just above a node on the same scape; usually, another flower spike will be produced.

P. amabilis is a large plant, with 20-inch-long leaves. It produces pure white flowers that are 5 inches across and spotted red.

Phalaenopsis stuartiana
Zumita

(Hausermann Orchids)

Phalaenopsis amabilis *hybrids: The white Phalaenopsis has been a favorite flower for years, and there has been constant hybridization.*

Opposite: Another of the fine Oncidium equitant hybrids—dwarf plants with flowers of wonderful colors.

(Hermann Pigors)

P. amboinensis has yellow sepals and petals barred with brown. The waxy, 2-inch flowers bloom in the spring and summer.

P. buyssonina, now known as *Doritis pulcherrima* var. *buyssonina*, has mottled green leaves 5 to 8 inches long. The flowers, about 2 inches across, are crimson-purple, the two lower sepals bordered with white.

P. schillerana, with marbled foliage, produces large, rose-purple flowers in the winter. The similarly colored lip is spotted red at the base.

P. stuartiana, with mottled foliage, has branched, many-flowered scapes of variable lengths. The upper sepals and petals are white. This orchid blooms in the winter.

P. violacea has cream-colored sepals and petals, with a deep shade of reddish purple on the innermost half. This is a summer bloomer.

White Phalaenopsis Hybrids

These hybrids are easy to grow in average home temperatures of 58°F at night, but they do require good air circulation. Diffused light suits the plants, and they prefer even moisture at their roots. Most white hybrids do not need a drying-out period. Feed your Phalaenopses regularly with Peters 30-10-10 plant food most of the year, but in the summer switch to Peters 10-30-20.

P. cornu-cervi has 2-inch, yellowish green flowers barred and blotched with red-brown and a whitish lip. This unusual orchid blooms in the summer.

P. esmeralda, also known as *Doritis pulcherrima*, has 6-inch-long, dark green leaves and bears delicate pink or rose flowers.

P. lueddemanniana, with leaves 6 to 10 inches long, produces magnificent 2-inch, white

Phalaenopsis schilleriana: While not producing as large a flower as its cousins, this species Phalaenopsis greets you with hundreds of flowers.

A true species, Phalaenopsis violacea has large broad leaves and small but endearing flowers of fine color.

(Hausermann Orchids)

flowers that are barred amethyst-purple in a circular pattern.

P. mannii, very handsome, has a golden yellow inflorescence blotched with brown, the lip light yellow fringed purple. This orchid likes cool temperatures, 54 to 62°F.

P. parishii is a dwarf variety, with leaves 2 to 4 inches long and white flowers spotted purple and overlayed with bright rose-purple; the fringed lip has a yellow-brown center.

P. rosea is a small plant with leaves about 8 inches long. It has tiny white or rose flowers.

Some newly introduced hybrids offer branching spikes with as many as 100 flowers to a plant. Here is a list of excellent winter- and spring-blooming white hybrids. (The last three hybrids are white with a red lip.)

Winter Maiden × Lafayette
Carl Hausermann × Winter Maiden AM/AOS
Winter Beauty 'York' AM/AOS
Barbara Lynn × Prairie du Chien
Prairie du Chien × Winter Beauty AM/AOS
Winter Maiden
Ice Sculpture

Cherryvale '#1' × Evangeline 'Exquisita' Cherryvale

Portola 'Mt. Madonna' × Muriel Turner 'Corcoran'

Portola 'Mt. Madonna' × Grace Palm '51'

Portola 'Mt. Madonna' × Norman Peterson x Polar Gull '#1'

Prairie du Sac × Mauston

Prairie du Sac × self

Cher Ann 'York' HCC/AOS × Mauston

Pink, Lavender, and Purple Phalaenopses

Pink Phalaenopses produce flowers of pale pink, deep rose, purple, and many shades between. The medium-sized flowers are smaller than those of the white Phalaenopses, and most varieties produce many, many blooms. Phalaenopsis Dorisellita × Hokuspokus × Phal. Monticello is a prime example of an exquisite pink Phalaenopsis. More so than the whites, some pinks have a branching habit contributed by Doritis lineage, but this may be a disadvantage because wildly branching types lose some elegance and beauty, and the busy branching pattern can assault the viewer's eye. Most of these plants are robust, with thick stems, and grow well with routine Phalaenopsis care. Most are at their bloom peak in early spring, but plants may also bloom in the autumn and winter.

Pink, lavender, and purple hybrids: Here are nine favorites of mine.

Uvaldo × Beard's Sunshine

Hokuspokus × Beard's Sunshine

Zauberrose × Lippstadt × Monticello

Dorisellita × Hokuspokus × Monticello Arlene Andrews

But Beautiful '#3' × Rose Girl '#1'

Sweet Dreams 'A3' × Zauberrot 'Largo'

Zauberrose '#1' × Diana '#1'

Zada's Best '#1 Pink Lip' × Zauberrose '#2 Dark'

Yellow Phalaenopses

The Phalaenopsis genus has a wide range of yellows. Some varieties are pale yellow; others, such as Hausermann's Phal. Gold Cup 'Everlasting,' are almost true yellow. Many of the plants have faint markings, such as brown dots and red bars.

The yellow Phalaenopses do not branch as much as the pinks, and stems are not usually as stout as those of the whites or pinks. Flowers may be small, to about 2 inches in diameter, or larger, about 5 inches across.

A very successful yellow Phalaenopsis hybrid from Hausermann Orchids.

Some varieties, such as Phal. Paula Hausermann 'Yellow Ribbon' AM/AOS, have a contrasting lip color, making the plants very appealing.

Most yellow Phalaenopses are not as easy to grow as other hybrids. Too much moisture affects them adversely, and they are weaker than the others. Bloom season is variable but usually at its peak in spring. I do not recommend these plants for beginners.

Yellow hybrids: Here are nine excellent choices.

Phal. Kewaunee × *Phal. amboinensis*
Sun Prairie 'Yellow Star'
Hausermann's Elegance × Wyocena
Paula Hausermann 'Sunshine' HCC/AOS
Golden Buddha × Hausermann's Elegance
Desert Wind

Gold Cut 'Everlasting'
Paula Hausermann 'Yellow Ribbon' AM/AOS
Golden Amboin

Red Phalaenopses

The colors of the red Phalaenopses are not as bright as they could be, but I believe that in time the hybridists will develop better ones. The heavy flowers are fairly large, to about 2 inches in diameter. Plants tolerate a range of temperatures (56°F at night) without harm and need little care.

Red hybrids: These plants bloom in the autumn or winter.

Phal. Winter Dawn × Phal. Luedde-Violacea × *Phal. fasciata* × *Phal. amboinensis*
Phal. Leudde-Violacea × *Phal. fasciata* 'Cherryvale' × Phal. Princess Kaiulani 'Carriage Hill' AM/AOS
Coral Isles 'York' AM/AOS × Golden Buddha 'Carriage Hill'
Carnival 'Bonsall' HCC/AOS × Golden Buddha 'Carriage Hill'
Princess Lorraine 'Flaming Star' HCC/AOS × Freed's Danseuse 'Treva' HCC/AOS
Phal. Coral Isles × *Phal. leuddemanniana* × Phal. Violet Charm
Dorisellita 'Midnight' HCC/AOS × Allspice 'Ft. Worth'
George Vasquez 'Flaming Glory' HCC/AOS × Freed's Danseuse 'Treva' HCC/AOS
Phal. gigantea × *Phal. mariae* × Phal. Malibu Imp 'Rieta' AM/AOS
Sophie Hausermann × Vitrail 'Bon Bon'
Red Wine 'Ruby' × George Vasquez 'Flaming Glory' HCC/AOS

Phalaenopsis Paula Hausermann
(Hausermann Orchids)

Penang 'York' AM/AOS × Coral Isles 'York'
AM/AOS

Diane Rigg 'Lista' × Spica 'Florence'
AM/AOS

Striped and Novelty Phalaenopses

This group includes the breathtaking candy-stripe hybrids, the exquisite spotted varieties such as Phal. Carnival 'Bonsall' AM/AOS, and an odd assortment of novelty colors: peach, copper with or without spots, and muted pastel shades blotched or reticulated.

These appealing Phalaenopses need little care, the same as that for the red Phalaenopsis. Most bloom when they are only 3 years old, and many, many varieties are inexpensive. These are excellent orchids for beginners because you almost cannot go wrong with them.

Striped and novelty hybrids: Here is a list of a few of the hundreds of winter- and spring-blooming plants in this category.

Painted Cave 'York' HCC/AOS—white flowers with red spots

Class President 'Willowbrook'—yellow flowers with bright red markings

Winter Carnival × Jean McFarlin—white flowers with spots and stripes

Magdalene Acker × Wyocena—peach-pink flowers

Carnival 'Bonsall' × Welcome Home—white flowers with lavender blotching

Gold Coin × Welcome Home—white flowers spotted with lavender

Amy Hausermann × Kewaskum—white flowers with stripes, dots

Donald Rigg 'Peaches' × Wyocena—peach-copper tones

Miniature Multiflora Phalaenopses

These lovely plants have variable bloom times.

Good Cheer 'Cutie' × Phal. schillerana 'Purpurea #1'

Good Cheer 'Cutie' × Giggles 'A'

Adeline Anderson 'Mimi' × Phal. schillerana 'Jungle Light'

Be Glad 'Santa Cruz' × Melinda Nan 'Jones' Be Glad

Cassandra 'Santa Cruz' × Larry Oberhaus '#1'

Be Glad '#1' × Pink Minuet 'Dark'

Little Kris 'Bright Future' × Malibu Frolic 'Pink Snow'

Memoria Lil Schrager 'Classic' × Be Glad 'Louisa'

Doritaenopsis (Doritis × Phalaenopsis)

The flowers of this cross are generally darker in color than those of Phalaenopsis and somewhat smaller, but there are many blooms to a scape. The colors—dark lavenders, fuschias—almost look crystalline; they literally glow. Most Doritaenopsis hybrids bear vertical stems in a very handsome candelabrum effect. The flowers stay in bloom for over 6 months.

Most varieties can tolerate coolness at night (55°F). Shade the plants from strong summer sun.

Doritaenopsis hybrids: These plants bloom in the winter and spring.

Junior Miss '#4' × Festivity 'Cutie'
Coral Gleam 'Samuel B. Mosher'
    FCC/AOS × *Phal. sumatrana* 'Red Knight'
    AM/AOS
Gorgeous Gold 'Canary' × Star of Florida
    'Princess'
Dainty Miss 'Pink Miss' × Melanie Beard
    'Bright Center'
Winneconne × Phal. Alfonso Ibarra
Pretty Nice 'York' AM/AOS
Ravenswood
Dtps. pulcherima 'Alba' × *Dtps. pulcherima*
    'Kodama Blue'
Dtps. pulcherima 'Kodama Blue' × self

Best of the Phalaenopses

Class President 'Addison Trail'—yellow flowers with rich red markings
Debbie Dramm 'Johnny'—candy-stripe flowers
Dorisellita 'Pink Delight'—rich red-purple flowers
Hausermann's Fireball—excellent red flowers
Paula Hausermann 'Yellow Sunset'—yellow flowers
Sun Prairie 'York' AM/AOS—yellow flowers
Winter Beauty 'York' AM/AOS—fine, large, white flowers
Winter Carnival 'Carousel'—white flowers with red blotches

RENANTHERA

With about a dozen species, Renantheras are from China, the Philippines, Indonesia, and Papua New Guinea. These plants can grow large, to 6 feet, and bear violent red, small flowers on long scapes—very dramatic. The genus is without pseudobulbs and features ascending stems of fleshy leaves and flower scapes produced from the leaf axils.

Grow the plants in full sun and keep the potting medium quite moist all year, except in winter, when the plants can be dried out somewhat. Renantheras will tolerate night temperatures of 50°F, if you have them outdoors.

R. imschootiana grows to 24 inches and has brilliant red flowers.

R. pulchella produces yellow flowers blotched with red.

Renanthera imschootiana
(Hermann Pigors)

Stanhopea

Stanhopea is a genus of more than 25 species native to Mexico, Peru, and Brazil. These are great orchids for growing in hanging containers and can tolerate 50°F at night. Flowers appear from the base of the plant, and the intricate structure of the inflorescence makes these epiphytes a curiosity, perfect for those seeking the unusual. The fascinating large flowers appear in lurid color combinations but last only a few days. *Stanhopea wardii, S. insignis,* and *S. oculata* bloom in August and September and always create a sensation; *S. tigrina* and *S. ecornuta* are other species of these easy-to-grow orchids.

Out of flower, the species all look so alike that it is difficult to distinguish them, and they often are sold under incorrect names. The oval pseudobulbs are 2 to 3 inches long

Stanhopea oculata

and bear a single, broad, dark green leaf 12 to 24 inches tall. The scape grows down, so the plants must be grown in open or bottomless containers. The flowers of many species are heavily scented. Some have the odor of menthol or camphor; *S. tigrina* has a powerful vanilla fragrance.

Always shade Stanhopeas. As mentioned, the plants do well in hanging containers; give them light but no sun, as in a north exposure. Most species react adversely to root disturbance, so repot only when absolutely necessary. Repot in tightly packed fir bark in large (10- to 12-inch) containers; occasionally add some fresh bark.

This genus thrives in warmth; never let nighttime temperatures in the winter drop below 50°F. High humidity (about 70 percent) and abundant moisture are needed during growth, at which time additional fertilizer will also be beneficial. In the winter decrease watering, but never let the bark become really dry.

S. wardii has yellow or white sepals and petals spotted red. The base of the complex lip is orange-yellow, with a purple-brown spot on each side. The flower color is variable in this species.

S. insignis has yellow flowers spotted purple, with a white lip blotched bright purple and a pair of fleshy horns.

S. oculata has a lemon-yellow inflorescence, with a narrow orange-yellow lip darkly spotted. Flower color is variable in this species.

S. tigrina bears the largest flowers in the genus, about 7 inches across, dull orange blotched purple, with a yellow lip.

S. ecornuta produces cream-white flowers, yellow-orange in the center and spotted purple.

Trichopilia

Trichopilias, from Mexico, Brazil, and Cuba, are stunning, large-flowered orchids often overlooked by hobbyists. The plants do very well in warm climates and bloom in late summer and fall. The genus is characterized by flat compressed pseudobulbs tipped by a single leaf. The short scapes, erect or pendant and with one to four flowers, are produced from the base of the pseudobulbs.

Above: Stanhopea wardii. *Bearing flowers from the bottom of the container, Stanhopeas remain a bizarre flowering species. Flowers last only a few days.*
(A. R. Addkison)

Left: Trichopilia suavis *bears unusually large flowers, many to a stem.*
(Hermann Pigors)

These orchids need light but not intense sun. They are intolerant of excess moisture, so water them only when the potting medium is dry. Occasionally soak the plants and let them dry out completely. Feed moderately. Protect from cold below 50°F.

T. suavis is about 14 inches tall, with creamy white, 6-inch flowers and twisted petals.

T. tortillis, the most popular species in the genus, has pale rose flowers about 6 inches across, sepals and petals twisted.

T. elegans produces small flowers, about 3 inches across and white.

Vanda

Vanda is a genus of epiphytic orchids native to the Far East, Malaysia, the Philippines, and the East Indies. Many hybrids are quite successfully grown in warm regions, including Hawaii and southern Florida where they can grow outdoors almost all year. Vandas are closely allied to the Aerides and Renantheras, and they need warmth and many hours of direct sun. Of the 70 known species, most are easy to grow and produce large, showy flowers in areas where moderate climates prevail year-round. However, *V. coerulea* will tolerate cooler temperatures and needs less sun, so I recommend this species for the beginner; *V. teres* and *V. suavis* are other good species.

Vandas must receive at least 6 hours of direct sun daily to produce flowers. Repot infrequently; when repotting, use large containers (8 to 12 inches in diameter) and large-grade fir bark.

V. coerulea bears pale blue flowers veined darker blue. They are about 4 inches across and appear in the late fall.

V. cristata is a small plant, about 9 inches high, with short scapes. It bears exquisite, 2-inch flowers whose sepals and petals are yellowish green, with lips streaked with red and white lines. Flowers last on the plant over 2 months.

V. parishii has leaves 6 to 9 inches long and produces several scented flowers that are 2 inches across and yellowish green spotted with red-brown.

Vanda orchids decorate a lath house, where they bloom profusely in dappled sunlight.

Pink, Red, and Strawberry Vandas

Vanda hybrids have recently blossomed all over the country because hybridists have made enormous gains with this genus. The pink and strawberry color varieties are the most popular. Most of these hybrids share Vanda Nellie Morley as their ancestor; they generally bloom in the fall and winter. The culture for these hybrids, which also include shades of red, is the same as for other Vandas.

Pink, red, and strawberry hybrids: The bloom seasons of these charming Vandas are the spring and summer for the pinks and strawberries, autumn and winter for the reds.

The typical purple coloring is seen in this old favorite Vanda, Vanda Omeana.

Vanda suavis
(A. R. Addkison)

V. roxburghii, about 24 inches tall, bears fragrant 2-inch, pale green flowers splotched with brown; the small lip is lined with white and has a violet-purple disk. This is easy to grow.

V. sanderiana, the queen of the Vandas, has large, handsome flowers 5 inches across and almost flat. The soft pink color is suffused with white, the lower petals yellow crossed with red veins. The intricate lip is tawny yellow streaked with red, the front part marked with chocolate brown.

V. suavis, with cream-white flowers spotted red-purple, is free-flowering. There are many hybrids, so flower color is varied.

V. teres has fleshy, pencil-like foliage. Flowers are pale rose or magenta. This species needs a definite rest in winter.

One of the many Ascocenda
*hybrids—magnificent colors
and so easy to grow in warm
climates. Most are very
floriferous.*
(A. R. Addkison)

Madame Rattana × Aurawan
Deva × Gordon Dillon
Josephine van Brero × Pimsai
Josephine van Brero × Madame Rattana
Memoria Louise Fuchs
Bhimayothin
Nellie Morley 'Red Berry' AM/AOS
Josephine van Brero × Linda 'Red'
Madame Rattana × Aurawan
Jennie Hashimoto 'Chaleo' × Renton
   Hutchinson 'Orchidglade'

Blue Vandas

These are the most popular within the
Vanda family. The numerous varieties produce a splendid array of flowers in shades of
blue, purple, and combinations of blue and
purple. The flowers of some varieties are
almost 6 inches across. These magnificent
plants are especially suitable for the
Southern states with daytime temperatures
of 80°F and cooler nights because the blue
Vandas thrive in such conditions.

Blue hybrids: These pretty orchids bloom
in the autumn and winter.

Gordon Dillon 'Sapphire'
Kasem's Delight 'Dark Blue' × Keeree
   'Chiengmai' AM/RHT
Madame Rattana 'Dark Red' × *V. caerulea*
   'Chiengmai'

Opposite: Ascocenda
(B. Kelly)

Ascocenda 'Sunburst'
(B. Kelly)

Rothschildiana
Springtime × *V. caerulea*
Fuch's Delight
Charungraks × *V. caerulea*
Onomea
Hilo Princess 'Alice' AM/AOS
Hilo Blue
Judy Miyamoto 'Blue Velvet' AM/AOS

Ascocenda Hybrids

The marriage of Ascocentrum and Vanda has produced a wonderful group of hybrids known as Ascocendas. These plants have flowers somewhat smaller than those of the Vandas, but they produce more flowers, as many as 20 to a stem. The color range is almost as varied as that among the Cattleyas, with orange, reds, pink, lavender, purple, and chartreuse types. Some bloom in the fall, but most Ascocendas are summer blooming, offering a wealth of color for little effort. Grow these orchids in slatted baskets because they need good air movement at their roots. Keep the plants very moist most of the year except in the winter, when they can be grown somewhat dry. Like the Vandas, the Ascocendas are ideal for warm climates because they prefer warm daytime temperatures.

Yellow Ascocenda hybrids: The bloom season for these orchids is variable.

Ascda. Pinas 'Coqui' AM/AOS × Yip Sum Wah 'Boynton' AM/AOS
Ascda. Borincana
Ascda. Pong 'Orchidglade' × *V. tessellata*

Ascda. Marion Perreira
Ascda. Sunkist 'Voodoo' AM/AOS × Capricorn 'Rainbow' FCC/AOS, SM/SFOS
Ascda. Salva Dela Pena
Ascda. Inthira
Ascda. Fuch's Gold
Ascda. 'Sunburst'

Peach Ascocenda hybrids: The bloom season is variable.

Ascda. Phairot × *V.* Charungraks
V. Eisensander × Ascda. Bonanza 'Bella Tew' AM/AOS

Ascda. Medasand × Madame Kenny
V. lamellata var. Boxallii × Ascda. Too Soon
 'Orchidglade' SM/7WOC

Orange Ascocenda hybrids: The bloom
season is variable.
Ascda. Medasand × *Ascda. miniatum*
V. Charungraks × Ascda. Madame Kenny
Ascda. Thonglor 'T. Orchids #2' × *Ascda.
 curvifolium*
Ascda. Bonanza 'Bella Tew' AM/AOS-HOS
Ascda. Yip Sum Wah 'Thai Treasure'
Ascda. Chaiyot 'Orange Crush'
Ascda. Peggy Foo

Pink Ascocenda hybrids: The bloom
season is variable.
Ascda. Fiftieth State Beauty 'Mayumi'
 AM/HOS
Ascda. Irene Van Aistyne
Ascda. Marlene Hinton
Ascda. Elizabeth Kendall
Ascda. Diane Fuchs
Ascda. Bonanza
Ascda. Cholburi

Blue Ascocenda hybrids: The bloom
season is variable.
Ascda. Lenachai × *V. caerulea*
Ascda. Bangkok Beauty
Ascda. Jean Ward
Ascda. David Parker

Vandas and Ascocendas decorate
this tree-top-like environment, and the
plants grow with gusto.

CHAPTER SEVEN

Orchids Outdoors

In the South we are blessed with an amenable climate that lets us grow certain orchids in the landscape; in pots hanging from trees, in lath houses or screened enclosures; or in containers on patios, porches, or terraces. In Zones 8 to 11, where temperatures rarely drop below 40°F, orchids can be outdoor decoration. These zones include the southern portions of Texas, Louisiana, Mississippi, Alabama, Georgia, South Carolina, North Carolina, and all of Florida. (Your microclimate may differ from the general zone designation.)

In Zones 8 to 11, dozens of orchids can grow outside, including Oncidiums and spray-type Epidendrums. Displayed in mass, many of the orchids are stunning subjects gardeners will welcome. Whether your landscape is in sun or shade, there are orchids for your outdoor use, depending on your lowest nighttime temperatures and occasional frosts.

In Pots

You can grow plants in pots or baskets and hang them from the lower limbs of trees or display them as spot decoration. Here in Florida, my porch is adorned with potted orchids year-round. And any indoor orchids you summer outdoors benefit greatly from rainwater and natural air currents: Growth is vigorous, and when returned indoors, the plants will be better able to endure any gray winter weather.

Spray-type Ansellias are perfectly suited to patio and atrium growing. The plants have long, erect branches crowded with small, yellow-and-brown flowers that last a long time. Outside, these plants grow rapidly. Sobralia, an uncommonly large orchid, does well for me outdoors on a south deck. It receives good sunlight most of the day, and the cool nights (40°F) do not seem to harm the plant. Try the species *S. macrantha*, but

Vanda orchids in a Naples, Florida garden; the mass of other plantings affords protection from direct sun and helps keep temperatures optimum on cold nights.

A free-flowering Dendrobium welcomes visitors to this Southern home.

remember that only mature plants bloom. *Laelia anceps* and *L. gouldiana* are also good orchids for growing in pots or mounted on bark outside. They bear lovely pink or lavender flowers in August and September. I also grow some smaller species of orchids on tree fern blocks fastened to my fence posts and trellis.

ℒᴀᴛʜ ℋᴏᴜꜱᴇꜱ

A lath house is an enclosed area constructed of battens or lathing (sold in bunches or strips), or 1 × 1-inch lumber spaced 2 inches apart to act as a roof. In this configuration, the laths filter the sun throughout the day; no direct sun hits the plants, which can kill most orchids quickly. Built properly, the average lath house is a beneficial place for

orchids. The structure can be left open or screened; the floor can be of cinders or stones. Ready-made trellis panels can also be fashioned into a quasi–lath house.

Slatted benches are necessary in any lath house to put flats within easy reach and to provide air to the bottoms of pots. Commercially made metal or wood greenhouse benches are expensive; it is much cheaper to build benches from 2 × 4s. Circulating fans are also necessary for keeping the air moving. Other necessities include a cooler or some apparatus for misting the orchids.

The temperature in the lath house will be less than the outdoor nighttime temperature, but this will not be enough protection from the weather if you live in Zone 7. In such a situation, use additional covering, such as plastic sheeting or rigid plastic panels to protect the plants during inclement nights.

ℐCREENED ℰNCLOSURES

The traditional and popular screened enclosure is beautiful and functional, but it is suitable for only certain orchids because in these structures, totally open to the elements, the nighttime temperature can drop quite low. The orchids that can be grown in a screened enclosure should be grown as hanging plants, with the containers suspended from vertical poles placed within the enclosure. Alternatively, grow the orchids in containers and place the containers on wooden benches within the enclosure.

The two obvious advantages of growing orchids in a screened enclosure is that the air movement is excellent; orchids thrive in a buoyant atmosphere. The disadvantage is

Temporary Lath House

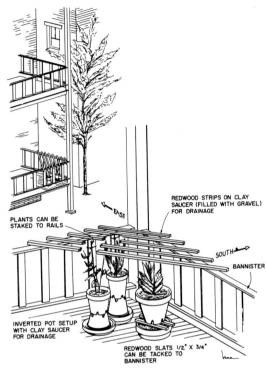

Left: The interior of the lath house, showing filtered light on Dendrobiums.
(A. R. Addkison)

that during low nighttime temperatures, the orchids are not protected from cold, in which case they must be moved indoors or moved against the house wall. If the cool spell lasts more than a few nights, you must protect the plants by putting sheets of burlap (sold at nurseries) over them at night.

If the screened enclosure faces west, you must provide some protection from the direct rays of the sun. Use free-standing trellises or awnings or other devices to thwart

year for the newly planted orchid to become established on the tree. Water the plant and tree fern slab heavily. You can grow almost any epiphytic orchid this way if your area receives enough sunlight and water.

In nature, many orchids grow in rocks, but placing them in such situations in the garden is difficult. The best method is to put them in a crevice or other space between two rocks. Use a thick layer of sphagnum moss under the plant and small stones or any other attaching device to anchor the moss and plant in place. All kinds of natural rock—pumice, granite, lava—can be used; avoid limestone or any other material that is too alkaline. Orchids growing on rocks need sunlight, buckets of water, and heavy feeding.

Gardens

In favored climates, terrestrial orchids such as Arachnis, Arundina, Bletia, and Habenaria can be grown directly in the ground in raised beds. Replace the existing soil with a mixture of sand, gravel, leaf mold, and pulverized fir bark.

Tall Oncidiums and Epidendrums planted in beds along a house wall or porch provide magnificent color almost year-round. Look for E. o'brienianum and its hybrids or the many O. leuochilum hybrids; these plants bear fine flowers by the dozens. Be sure the growing medium contains some charcoal, lava rock (in packages at nurseries), or some sterile, porous material so drainage is almost perfect. You can also use medium-grade fir bark.

Many of the orchids in this screened enclosure are grown in baskets so air can reach the plants' roots. Cattleyas as well as Vandas and Dendrobiums are grown this way.

the brutal rays. In an east or north situation, no problem exists. In a south exposure, watch plants to see whether the sun affects them adversely.

Growing Orchids on Trees or Rocks

Orchids grown on trees or rocks are unusual, easy to care for after their initial installation, and always elicit comment. Use a rough-bark tree, such as an oak, with a heavy crown of leaves. Plant your orchid in a tree fern slab, then tightly attach the slab to the tree with galvanized wire (or nail or staple it to the tree); there should be no movement of the slab. It will take several months to a

Some of the jewel orchids, grown for their richly marked foliage, thrive in the garden. *Goodyera pubescens* and *Haemeriadawsoniana* are inexpensive and readily available. They need shade, lots of moisture, and a free-draining compost. Rhyncostylis species can also be used in the garden; most are large plants and carry heavy spikes of dazzling flowers. They grow quickly with plenty of water and ample sunshine. The deciduous Dendrobiums, popular as houseplants, are also excellent outdoors.

In the garden, you can place potted orchids wherever you want them. Outdoor container orchids, whether in the garden or on porches, patios, or terraces, should not be set directly on the ground. Exceptions include Sobralias, Habenerias, and Pleiones, which can be sunk in their pots in the ground.

Watering and Insect Protection

Outdoors, orchids need plenty of water because sun and natural air currents evaporate moisture quickly. If rain is sparse, water daily during sunny days; generally, the orchids will be dry by evening. Grow the orchids in sheltered areas that receive dappled sunlight. Most orchids like some sun but, as mentioned, very few like direct sun. A few hours of sun a day is enough for most orchids grown outdoors.

Orchids are so tough that you should not have too many problems with insects. If you do, follow the advice given in Chapter 4 for indoor orchids.

The beautiful Epidendrum o'brienianum *brings bright orange color to the outdoors.*

An outdoor arbor in Sarasota, Florida where orchids thrive— a truly tropical scene.

WINTER PROTECTION FOR PLANTS

Protecting your orchids outdoors involves a few minutes of work, but it is necessary if temperatures drop into the 40s. A few nights of such temperatures most likely will not harm your orchids, but three or more nights of low temperatures can kill some. You must cover the plants with plastic, tarps, boxes, newspapers—any material that will shelter them from the effects of the cold.

Any orchids growing near the house will have some natural protection from the cold because temperatures near a building are somewhat warmer than those in the open. Orchids hanging from trees also receive some slight protection from the leafy branches of the trees. To protect orchids growing in containers outdoors, merely move the containers into the home.

In many of our Southern states, January and February are the months the temperatures are most likely to drop into the 40s or, on occasion, lower. By April, freezing weather is over, with nighttime temperatures in the 50s and 60s. For outdoor orchids, remember that a few nights of cold weather—say, 42 to 50°F—will not harm them. More than five or six nights of such weather, though, indicates that protection for plants is necessary. Whenever the temperature drops below 40°F, cover the plants. Burlap (sold at garden stores) and tarpaulins (at hardware stores) are easy-to-use plant protection; merely drape them over plants like a blanket. If using newspapers, fashion them into paper tents and secure them to the ground with sticks. Cut apart cardboard boxes and set them around plants. If you cover orchids with plastic bags, always poke a few holes in the bags so air can circulate, because plastic is nonporous.

Plants can take a beating from winds but are usually not harmed to any extent. In 1993, when a storm brought 60-mile-per-hour winds, I lost a few leaves on my orchids, but that was the only damage.

Watery foliage and stems indicate that your outdoor orchid has suffered from cold temperatures. Cut away the injured parts with a sterile knife and move the ailing orchid indoors. Water the plant very little, and do not feed it. You must wait until the orchid has regained some of its vigor before you resume routine watering and feeding.

Orchids here are suspended from trees in an outdoor terrace. Orchids under trees are afforded some protection from low temperatures.

ℱEEDING

Indoors, orchids need a routine feeding program to prosper. Outdoors, orchids can survive with less fertilization because rains and even the wind carry nutrients to the plants (the wind picks up assorted decaying matter). However, some feeding is in order even for outdoor-growing orchids. Use Peters orchid food (30-20-10) during the spring and summer months; apply the food once every 2 to 3 weeks. Apply it as you would for indoor orchids: Sprinkle the food (it is in powder form) on the fir bark and water it in thoroughly.

℘LANT ℋARDINESS ℤONE ℳAP

The Plant Hardiness Zone Map, which is published by the United States Department of Agriculture, helps determine which garden plants will grow in which areas (zones) of the country. The map is based on average annual low temperatures and is essentially used when choosing outdoor flowers, shrubs, and trees with various levels of cold-hardiness. This book is concerned with the geographical parts of the country that fall into Zones 7, 8, 9, 10, and 11 (Zone 11, the southernmost tip of Florida, was recently added):

Zone 7:	0 to 10°F	Parts of Texas; Oklahoma, Arkansas, Tennessee, North Carolina, Virginia
Zone 8:	10 to 20°F	Southern Texas; Louisiana, Mississippi, Alabama, South Carolina, Georgia
Zone 9:	20 to 30°F	Parts of Texas; Louisiana, northern Florida
Zone 10:	30 to 40°F	Southern Florida
Zone 11:	40 to 50°F	Parts of southern Florida

This map is certainly helpful, but it is not mandatory because various climatic features can vary 5 miles apart outdoors due to topography, buildings, and other factors. You're the best judge of your particular microclimate.

ℳNSELLIA

Zones 9, 10, 11

These little-known orchids include only a few species, all native to tropical Africa. The plants have long, tapered pseudobulbs that are almost like canes, and the dark green leaves are somewhat leathery. The numerous 2-inch, vivid yellow-and-brown flowers make a natural bouquet.

Ansellias are easy to grow and adapt to outdoor culture in many areas; they will tolerate a few nights of 40°F temperature. They can be grown as garden orchids in soil or in equal parts of soil and bark. Protect the plants from the elements by placing them close to the home (or they can be grown indoors). These orchids like bright light with some sun and need feeding; use Peters 20-30-10 during growth in the spring and summer. Flowers appear in the summer. Only one species is offered, but various forms of the species are available.

A. africana, sometimes known as *A. gigantea* or *A. nilotica*, produces sprays of beautiful,

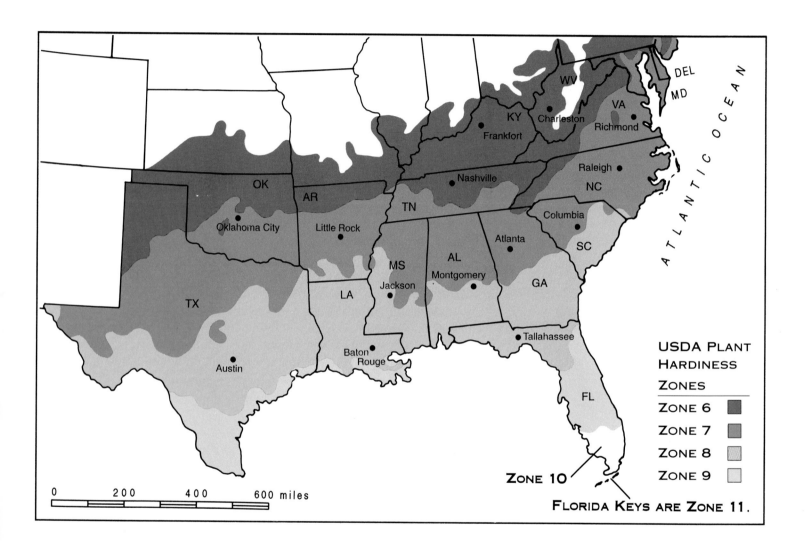

ATLANTIC OCEAN

DEL
MD
WV
KY
Charleston
VA
Richmond
Frankfort
Raleigh
NC
OK
AR
Nashville
TN
Oklahoma City
Little Rock
Columbia
SC
Atlanta
AL
MS
Montgomery
Jackson
LA
GA
TX
Tallahassee
Baton Rouge
Austin
FL

USDA PLANT HARDINESS ZONES
ZONE 6
ZONE 7
ZONE 8
ZONE 9

ZONE 10
FLORIDA KEYS ARE ZONE 11.

0   200   400   600 miles

vivid yellow-and-brown flowers that last 2 to 3 weeks.

ARACHNIS

Zones 8, 9, 10, 11

Arachnis is a genus of 15 species growing from the Himalayas to New Guinea. Some species are tall-stemmed with leathery leaves; others are short-stemmed. All species are free-flowering. A healthy plant may have 30 multicolored flowers.

These orchids can be grown successfully in pots, but they do even better when planted in raised beds of garden loam and sand. The plants need full sun for bloom, and they must have heavy watering and some fertilizing.

A. clarkei is about 6 feet tall, with yellow sepals and petals barred with chestnut brown.

A. flos-aeris (moschifera) grows to 14 feet in height. The leathery leaves are about 8 inches long. The flower scape is usually branching, with greenish white or yellow flowers blotched with chocolate red and faintly scented. This Arachnis blooms for a long time.

ARUNDINA

Zones 9, 10, 11

Arundina is a genus of splendid orchids from southern China and the Himalayas. Grow the plants in raised beds of rich garden loam and give them plenty of water, warmth, humidity, and sunlight. If you grow this orchid in a pot, do not expect the rose-colored flowers to appear for many years.

A. graminifolia has reedlike stems 24 to 80 inches high and grassy leaves. The deliciously fragrant flowers, produced from a terminal stem, are 2 to 3 inches across, with sepals and petals light rose, the lip rose, the front lobe deep purple, and the throat white and lined with orange. A mature plant blooms for several months in the summer.

BLETIA

Zones 8, 9, 10, 11

Bletia, with about 50 species, is a genus native to the United States. It is also found in Mexico, Peru, the West Indies, and Central America. These lovely terrestrial orchids can be quite spectacular. They are easy to find (some are even sold packaged at supermarkets) and inexpensive. The plants will adapt to pot culture. They are easy to grow, and the flowers can be used for cut flowers indoors.

The leaves are grassy, and flowers are borne on the top of wandlike stems from the base of the cormlike bulb. The flowers, usually rose, lilac, or purple, are 1 to 2 inches in diameter. They last only a few days but are quickly replaced by new blooms, so a plant can be in bloom for about 6 weeks.

Bletias need a sandy, rich soil and shade. In growth, they require plenty of water. After the plants flower, let them die down naturally and carry them barely moist until they show signs of growth. Dealers have the corms in stock in the fall and winter.

B. hyacinthina has grassy foliage about 3 feet long and 1-inch, rose-purple flowers.

B. b. alba has white flowers. Both are hardy to 32°F.

B. purpurea usually has 6 to 12 pink or rose flowers about 1¹/₂ inches across. The flowers do not expand fully, and the petals form an open hood over the lip. This is an easy-to-grow orchid.

CALOPOGON

Zones 7, 8, 9, 10, 11

Calopogon is a genus of deciduous and hardy orchids that can also be grown in pots indoors in a cool location. These terrestrial orchids grow about 20 inches tall, with grassy foliage and vivid purple flowers about 1 inch in diameter.

C. pulchellus has wiry scapes of purple flowers with a tufted lip. It blooms in the

The Calopogons are generally deciduous orchids that make excellent garden plants. This is C. pulchellus, *which bears solitary flowers on medium-tall spikes. It can be difficult to grow.*

(Hermann Pigors)

autumn. Grow this species in a well-drained compost of loam, leaf mold, and sand in a moist and shady location. This is a difficult but not impossible orchid to grow.

CALYPSO

Zones 7, 8, 9, 10, 11

Calypso is a genus of exquisitely beautiful terrestrial orchids that bear a solitary flower. Grown from a tuber, a Calypso has a network of fleshy roots. The blossom is terminal at the top of an erect spike. Calypsos achieve their best effect when grown in small groups.

These charming garden orchids need shade, dampness, and coolness. Grow them in a light, sandy soil with leaf mold, at a 3-inch depth.

C. borialis (bulbosa), an endangered species, is available from growers who have propagated plants in the United States. It has a solitary, dark green leaf and a slender stem bearing a fragrant lilac-and-purple flower. About 1 inch across, the flower features narrow and spreading deep purple parts, the lip white and dotted with red-purple. If you cannot grow this plant in the garden, pot a tuber and grow it indoors.

HABENARIA

Zones 9, 10

Habenaria is a very large genus, with more than 1,000 species. It is widely scattered throughout the temperate and tropical regions of the world. These deciduous terrestrial orchids bear many exquisite flowers shaped like soaring birds. The plants can be a few inches to 4 feet high. They have erect and leafy stems, and the blossoms are produced in long and dense or few-flowered spikes or racemes.

Give Habenarias a terrestrial, sandy soil similar to an African violet mixture. The plants need sun and excessive moisture. To protect the plants from damping off, apply an antifungus chemical in the early stages of their growth.

H. radiata has grassy foliage with several large and magnificent, creamy white flowers with a green spur; it blooms in July and August. Grow the plant in a rich and sandy loam.

$\mathscr{P}$HAIUS

Zones 8, 9, 10

Phaius is a genus of large and showy terrestrial orchids from China, Africa, and Madagascar. These plants may lose their leaves in their second year, but growth starts again after a few months. Most Phaius orchids adapt to varying temperatures without difficulty. Most species of this genus have short pseudobulbs sheathed by the leaf bases and hardly distinguishable. The leaves are often more than 4 feet high. The erect flower spikes are produced from the base of the pseudobulbs. A healthy plant can put out 10 to 20 large, long-lasting, scented flowers that sometimes are 5 inches across.

These plants require filtered sunlight. Give them watering and heavy feeding up to the time the flowers actually open, then give them a good rest. During the resting period, dry out the compost slightly. Thrips (tiny, wingless insects) may infest Phaiuses, so check your plants periodically. See Chapter 4 for a preventative.

P. grandifolius, often sold at flower shows, produces dozens of large, multicolored flowers that are first pale in color, then later darken considerably. The sepals and petals are yellow-brown and silver-hued, the lip rose-purple and whitish with a blue spot in the center. Grow in a rich soil and give these plants plenty of water and some sun.

P. maculata has a somewhat smaller inflorescence, handsome, golden yellow flowers, and dark green leaves spotted yellow. This plant needs protection below 52°F.

Phaius grandifolius *has tall stalks of flowers that can be cut for indoor decoration.*

Although seldom seen, Phaius maculatus is a terrestrial that is easy to grow outdoors in warm weather. You can leave the plants in the ground all year—they die back somewhat after blooming but, similar to bulbous plants, start up again later with new growth.

PLEIONE

Zones 8, 9, 10, 11

Pleione is a genus of about 20 species of spectacular terrestrial orchids from the Himalayas, southeast Asia, China, and Taiwan. The plants are grown from corms, which are sold in plastic bags at supermarkets. The plants also thrive indoors.

Pleiones have angular pseudobulbs topped with thin, pale green foliage. The leaves rarely grow longer than 10 inches, and the vivid purple flowers, some 4 inches in diameter, are mammoth for the size of the plant.

These orchids must have perfect drainage, so use a mix of equal parts of fir bark, leaf mold, and sharp white sand. Be sure the garden bed is raised about 4 inches, so water can run off easily. Plant the bulbs while it is still cool outside, 45°F. Put the bulbs in a protected area that receives some bright light. Water the plants sparingly for the first few weeks until growth is well under way. Then, when the roots are actively growing, give the plants plenty of water. When the leaves have fully developed (the end of the summer for most species), decrease watering to perhaps only once a week until the buds form. Generally, foliage will die at this time, and watering can then be increased to bring the plants to full bloom. The bloom times are late autumn and winter. Most Pleiones are hardy to 32°F.

P. bookeriana, with foliage about 5 inches high, produces leaves and flowers at the same time. The flowers are rose-colored, almost purple, with a brown-purple splotch on the lip. This species blossoms in the spring.

P. bumilis bears 3-inch, blush-white flowers spotted with amethyst-purple. The lip is handsomely fringed. This is a stellar orchid, also excellent for pot culture.

P. lagenaria is somewhat larger, with rose-lilac flowers that are stunning in the winter.

P. maculata is about 12 inches tall and produces 4-inch white flowers. The sepals and petals are streaked with purple. This orchid takes time and attention to bring into flower.

P. praecox, with 3-inch, rose-purple blooms, is somewhat more difficult to bring into bloom than the others listed here. Give it more sunlight than the other Pleiones.

Opposite: Overlooked, but certainly beautiful, are the many Pleione orchids. This is the white form, Pleione formosa—a stunning sight.

P. pricei, with leaves about 6 inches long, bears a solitary, 4-inch, pale rose flower with a large, white-fringed lip.

ℛHYNCOSTYLIS

Zones 10, 11

Known as the Foxtail Orchid because the flower scape is crowded with small flowers and looks like a fox's tail, this is generally an indoor plant. However, Rhyncostyles do so well outdoors in the warm months that I am including them in this chapter. From the Philippines, these plants are allied to the Vandas; only a few species are known. Grow the plants in fir bark in baskets suspended from trees or eaves. Wonderfully fragrant flowers are produced in the spring. Water

Rhyncostylis orchids moderately, and feed them only a few times a year.

R. gigantea is sometimes grown under the name Saccolobium. The plant has stout stems, heavy roots, and spatula-shaped, leathery leaves. The waxy flowers are usually pink or blush-white and spotted. It blooms in the fall and winter.

R. retusa is smaller than *R. gigantea*, to about 2 feet. The hundreds of small, fragrant flowers, usually blush pink or pink with spots, appear in the summer.

𝒮OBRALIA

Zones 10, 11

This is an overlooked genus of extremely fine garden orchids that grow about 6 feet tall and carry attractive, grassy foliage. There are about 35 species in the region extending from Mexico to Peru and Brazil. The beautiful and huge cerise flowers resemble those of the Cattleyas but do not have the same staying power, lasting only a few days. The flowers are followed by other flowers for several weeks in the summer, however.

Grow Sobralias in containers or very well-drained areas, and use a houseplant or outdoor soil mix. Flood plants with water during the warm months, and fertilize them a few times each month because they are greedy feeders. Plants like sun and resent having their roots disturbed, so repot those in containers only when absolutely necessary. Sobralias grown in the ground can be left alone to multiply on their own. Sobralias

A species from India, Rhyncostylis gigantea *bears dozens of small, sweetly scented flowers on long pendent stems.*
(A. R. Addkison)

Rhyncostylis retusa, *the foxtail orchid, bears pendent scapes of small flowers. From afar, the inflorescence resembles a bushy fox tail.*

can take some cold, but not extreme temperatures. On very cold nights (45°F or below), cover the plants with burlap or newspaper. If you are growing these orchids in containers, move them inside during nights below 50°F.

S. decora has fragrant, 3-inch, white or blush white flowers, with a rose-purple lip streaked with yellow.

S. macrantha grows to 8 feet, with reedlike growth, attractive leaves, and mammoth (8-inch), lavender flowers.

SPATHOGLOTTIS

Zones 10, 11

Spathoglottis is a genus of 10 species of terrestrial orchids distributed throughout the

Sobralia macrantha has grassy leaves and bears flowers up to 7 inches across in the summer. Plants can be grown in the ground—they may die down during the year, but they will come back again.
(Robert Read)

(opposite) Another terrestrial orchid from China, Spathoglottis unguiculata bears stunning violet-red blooms and has grassy, ribbed leaves. This deciduous orchid is related to Phaius and Calanthe.

East, from Burma to China and Hong Kong and some islands in the Pacific. This genus is allied with Phaius and Calanthe. The plants have small, cormlike pseudobulbs with tall, grassy foliage. The beautiful flowers, produced on the top of erect stems, are yellow or rose-purple.

Grow these orchids in a rich soil laced with sand. They need good sunlight and heavy watering, except after blooming, when a short rest is desirable. If growing these plants in pots, provide ample drainage material at the bottoms of the containers.

S. aurea has leaves 2 to 3 feet long and 3-inch, yellow flowers, the lip flushed with red. It is spring-blooming.

S. plicata, with leaves to 3 feet long, has erect flower stalks with 1- to 2-inch blooms, the sepals and petals violet-red, the lip bright yellow. It is summer-blooming.

These plants can tolerate temperatures in the 40s.

*Dendrobiums make great
cut flowers and last
for weeks in a vase of water.*

CHAPTER EIGHT

Orchids as Cut Flowers

Any flowers in the home add cheer to the room, but orchids also supply that something extra, that touch of class. During the past few years, home magazines have displayed cut orchids in interiors because the editors know that orchids indeed do "make" a room. Orchids are also becoming more and more popular as cut flowers because many of them stay fresh in water for 2 to 3 weeks, far outlasting the bloom of other favorite flowers, such as roses.

Die-hard orchid hobbyists will not like this section of the book because they find it very difficult to cut orchid flowers from the plants. But I assure you that most plants will not be harmed. In fact, in some cases, removing the flower helps the orchid by eliminating some of the stress on the plant. However, you just cannot cut any orchid. For example, Miltonias, Vandas, and certain other orchids do not fare well when cut and may last only a few days after their flowers have been removed. On the other hand, the flowers of such orchids as Oncidium, Phaius, Dendrobium, Phalaenopsis, and Epidendrum will last and last in a vase of water.

The Best Orchids for Cutting

Dendrobium

The reed-stemmed Dendrobiums, with long sprays of white or purple flowers, are elegant and attractive. Display the flowers by themselves in a tall vase, or insert them into floral arrangements for accent. Any of the Phalaenopsis- or antelope-type Dendrobiums are fine to use for cut flowers.

Epidendrum

These spray-type orchids with long stems are tiny replicas of Cattleyas. The colors of the flowers range from pink to brownish pink, and the flowers last about 2 weeks in

water. The Epidendrums are most effective when one or two are exhibited in a vase or when several are used as accents in large bouquets of garden flowers. *E. prismatocarpon, E. radicans,* and *E. stamfordianum* are all excellent species for cut flowers.

Oncidium

The best Oncidium species to use as cut flowers are *O. spathalaceum, O. splendidum,* and *O. leuchochilum.* These spray-type orchids have long stems, with dozens of flowers to a stem. The flower colors, rose and yellow, are beautiful; when displayed singly in a vase, the orchid flower paints a handsome picture.

Phaius

Mainly an outdoor orchid, Phaius offers dramatic beige and brown flowers on tall stalks. The flowers are excellent for use in a floral arrangement and last about 10 days. The best Phaius orchids for cut flowers are *P. maculatus* and *P. tankervillae.*

Opposite: Oncidium sphacelatum × *Oda Lippstern is a cross between the favorite* O. sphacelatum *and an Odontoglossum that produces larger flowers than the original Oncidium.*
(William Shaban)

Oncidium ampliatum *offers large sprays of yellow orchids for cut flower display.*

Phalaenopses

Phalaenopsis flowers are the orchids most often featured in design magazines, usually in their containers, although they also make excellent cut flowers. The arching sprays of white or pink butterflylike flowers last about 2 weeks in water. Dozens of Phalaenopsis varieties are suitable for cut flowers, but the best are those with white or pink flowers.

ORCHIDS AS DECORATIVE ACCENTS

As mentioned, currently the most popular interior orchid is Phalaenopsis, displayed in its container. But any orchid grown in a container is suitable for interior design, adding color and sophistication to living areas. Be sure to put a protective coaster or a piece of felt under any container so water does not seep through the container and onto furniture. All containers need such protection.

Water indoor orchids about once a week. If you have moved a potted orchid from its growing area, such as the garden room or the windowsill, move it back to its "home" after 2 or 3 weeks. Displaying an orchid elsewhere longer, keeping it out of the sun and without the frequent waterings it receives in its regular habitat, may harm the orchid.

A typical Phalaenopsis amabilis hybrid, the famous cut flower orchid.

Opposite: An arrangement of cut Dendrobium flowers; they last for weeks in a vase of water.

125

Afterword

We all now realize how valuable and dear our plants in the wild are, thanks to the dedication and care of members of the environmental movement. Orchids, especially, are being destroyed brutally in the world's rain forests, and farming and logging continue to kill off orchids in various other parts of the world as well. Indeed, the decimation of orchids has been so intense that recently CITES (Convention on International Trade in Endangered Species) has put most orchids on the endangered or threatened list. Thus, do not try to smuggle in any orchids from lands you have traveled to. If you do not care about the orchids, care about your pocketbook: The fine for importing orchids is extremely stiff.

Another effective measure against the loss of orchids has been the ban on the importation of orchids into almost all countries (this ban includes nursery stock orchids). Fortunately, most of the mail-order orchid growers and suppliers saw this problem coming and, through the wonders of propagating wild species that were brought into the United States years ago, have prevented any shortage of orchids.

It will be beneficial to join the American Orchid Society. Annual fees entitle you to their *Bulletin*, which contains much valuable orchid information.

Let us always keep in mind that the orchids in our homes and gardens are indeed gifts from nature: Take care of them, keeping them safe and healthy for our enjoyment and the enjoyment of others after us.

Most Commonly Asked Questions

Why do the buds on my orchids shrivel and drop?
Bud drop usually is caused by a sudden fluctuation in temperature, toxic salts in the potting medium, or not enough humidity in the air.

Can too much plant food result in many leaves and few flowers?
Yes, if the food has a high nitrogen content. Use a general plant food (30-10-10 or 20-10-10) for a few months, then switch to 10-30-20 for the rest of the year.

Why do leaf tips on some orchids die back? Is this serious?
No. The dieback is caused by too much fertilizer. Leach out the plants every month by taking them to the sink and running water through them for a few minutes.

Why has mildew attacked some of my orchids?
If night temperatures are cool (in the 50s) and humidity too high, botrytis can occur. Keep air moving in the growing area (use a small fan), and maintain nighttime temperatures a few degrees warmer.

How do you get rid of mealybugs?
Use alcohol on a cotton swab or cotton ball.

What are the rules for growing orchids under artificial lights?
Orchids need excellent air circulation, a difference in day and night temperatures, and, most importantly, the correctly timed light sequence. For example, some orchids need 13 hours under lights, others 14. Consult a good book on growing plants under artificial light.

Can the gas from the fireplace harm orchids?
Not if there is sufficient air circulation in the room. But plants too close to a fire may suffer from heat buildup.

What are some easy orchids to grow on a windowsill?
Phalaenopses are ideal because they can tolerate some low light, if necessary. Paphiopedilums are other good orchids.

What is some good general advice for getting Cattleyas to bloom?
Give Cattleyas somewhat cool (about 58°F) nighttime temperatures. If that doesn't work, check the heritage of the parents. If the parents were cool- or warm-growing, adjust temperatures accordingly.

Why do some of the backbulbs on my Cattleyas turn brown and die?
Backbulbs usually do die off after several years.

Why do some of my Cattleyas send up sheaths with no buds inside?
Be patient: Many Cattleyas initiate sheaths and then take several months to form buds.

Why do the flowers of my Cattleyas get smaller every year?
You probably have less than ideal light conditions. Try your Cattleyas in a greenhouse with optimum light.

What is the best kind of water for my Cattleyas?
Rainwater, but, of course, it is hard to collect. If you can drink the water from your tap, that water is fine for your plants, unless the tap water has too much chlorine. In this case, let a bucket of the water stand overnight before using it to water your plants.

What does the term "art shade" mean in regard to Cattleyas?
The term refers to pastel colors such as peach, apricot, and rust, and color ranges in between, as opposed to white or lavender.

Should Cattleyas rest after being repotted, or can they be watered as usual?
Give the plants a few days' rest before resuming normal watering, and at least a few weeks' rest before feeding them.

How can I overcome my trouble getting Oncidiums to bloom?
Give your Oncidiums excellent light, and be sure the potting medium is never too wet. Hybrid Oncidiums with Odontoglossum heritage need somewhat cool nights (55°F) to bloom.

What is the secret of getting Phalaenopses to rebloom?
Cut the spikes above a growing node after the top flowers fade. Usually the plants will rebloom in a few months.

Why are the lower leaves of my Phalaenopsis turning limp?
Stop watering the orchids so much, and reduce humidity in the air. However, occasionally the lower leaves of mature Phalaenopses do naturally fade and die back.

Why don't my Vandas bloom regularly, and why have some not bloomed in years although the leaves have not died?
To bloom regularly, Vandas need very high light intensity, which most homes lack. Try Ascocenda hybrids, which bloom with somewhat less light, and twice a year in good conditions.

Orchid Charts

Quick-Reference Orchid Chart

Full sun: 6–8 hours   Dappled sun: 2–3 hours   Half-sun: 3–4 hours

Semishade: 1–2 hours   Shade: light, no sun

Name	Plant size (inches)	Flower color	Flower size (inches)	Time of bloom	Suggested exposure
AERIDES					
crassifolium	7–12	amethyst purple	1–2	summer	half-sun
fieldingii	24–40	white mottled with purple	1½	various	full sun
japonicum	3–5	white marked red	1	summer	half-sun
maculosum	7–10	pale rose spotted purple	1	summer	half-sun
multiflorum	9–18	deep rose	1	summer	half-sun
odoratum	12–40	creamy white	1	various	full sun
ANGRAECUM					
eburneum	14–20	white	4	winter	semishade
philippinense	10–12	white	3	winter	semishade
leonis	10–12	white	2	winter	semishade
sesquipedale	30–40	white	6	winter	semishade
veitchii	24–36	white	7	winter	semishade
ANSELLIA					
africanus (gigantea)	24–30	yellow with brown spots	2–3	summer	half-sun

Note: Some orchids listed in these charts are not discussed in the book.

Name	Plant size (inches)	Flower color	Flower size (inches)	Time of bloom	Suggested exposure
ARACHNIS *Clarkei*	24–30	yellow-brown	2–3	summer	sun
ARUNDINA *graminifolia*	24–80	magenta	3–4	summer	sun
ASOCENDA (hybrids)	12–20	lavender-blue	2–3	summer	half-sun
ASCOCENTRUM					
curvifolium	10–14	magenta	1	spring	half-sun
miniatum	2–3	orange	1/2	spring	full sun
BLETIA					
hyacinthina	14–36	dark rose	2	summer	half-sun
purpurea	40–48	rose	1	summer	half-sun
BRASSAVOLA					
cucullata	5–7	white spotted red	2–4	various	full sun
digbyana	8–15	greenish white	5–7	various	full sun
glauca	5–2	greenish white	3	spring	half-sun
nodosa	6–9	white spotted red	2–4	various	full sun
BRASSIA			(length)		
caudata	16–24	light green tinted yellow, spotted brown	5–8	various	full sun
gireoudiana	8–16	yellow and brown	5–7	various	full sun
maculata	15–22	greenish yellow, spotted brown	6–9	summer	full sun
CALOPOGON *pulchellus*	18–20	purple	1–2	spring	semishade
CALYPSO *borialis*	8–10	purple	1	summer	semishade
CALANTHE					
masuca	20–30	dark violet	1	summer	dappled sun
rosea	10–14	variable; white to dark rose	1	winter	half-sun
veratrifolia	20–30	usually white	2	various	half-sun
vestita	10–14	cream white or pink shades	1	winter	half-sun

Name	Plant size (inches)	Flower color	Flower size (inches)	Time of bloom	Suggested exposure
CATTLEYA					
aclandiae	6–10	olive green, blotched purple	3–4	summer	full sun or half-sun
amethystoglossa	36	pale pink spotted dark pink		autumn	half-sun
bicolor		greenish lavender	3	fall	half-sun
bowringiana	40	pink-cerise	3	spring	half-sun
citrina	6–10	bright yellow with white lip	2–3	spring, summer	full sun or half-sun
dolosa	8–10	rose-magenta	3	autumn	half-sun
forbesii	12–16	greenish yellow	3–4	various	half-sun
harrisoniae		pale pink		summer	half-sun
luteola	5–9	pale yellow	2	summer	half-sun
nobilior	6–11	rose-magenta	3–4	various	half-sun
skinneri	12–26	rose-purple	2–3	spring	full sun
velutina		orange-brown	2–3	spring	half-sun
CYPRIPEDIUM (leaf spread)					
bellatulum	9–12	pale yellow spotted with maroon	2–3	various	semishade
concolor	6–8	yellow with crimson dots	2–3	summer	semishade
insigne	8–12	apple green, veined brown	4–5	various	semishade
niveum	6–8	white, dotted	3–4	summer	semishade
DENDROBIUM					
aggregatum	4–8	vivid yellow	1	spring	full sun
chrysotoxum	12–30	white, orange lip	1–2	spring	full sun
dalhousieanum	24–72	yellow and rose	3–4	spring	half-sun
densiflorum	20–36	orange-yellow	1–2	spring	full sun
fimbriatum	20–38	orange-yellow	2–3	various	half-sun
jamesianum	12–20	white with yellow-red throat	4–5	spring	half-sun
nobile hybrids	12–36	blush white with lavender tips, lip	3–4	winter, spring	half-sun in growth; full sun when leaves fall
phalaenopsis	12–36	lavender	2–4	various	full sun
pierardii	18–72	pale lavender	2–3	spring	half-sun
superbum	24–72	lavender	4–5	winter, spring	half-sun in growth; full sun when leaves fall
thyrsiflorum	14–30	white	1½–2	spring	half-sun
wardianum	24–30	white tipped purple	2–3	winter, spring	half-sun

Name	Plant size (inches)	Flower color	Flower size (inches)	Time of bloom	Suggested exposure
EPIDENDRUM					
aromaticum	14–18	greenish yellow	1½–1	spring	full sun
atropurpureum	14–18	greenish purple and brown	1–2	early spring	full sun
elegans	12–18	dark rose	2	winter	half-sun
fragrans	18–32	vivid yellow striped purple	2–3	summer	full sun
mariae	14	green and white	2	summer	full sun
nemorale	14	blush pink	2	winter	full sun
nocturnum	10–16	greenish white	3–4	winter	half-sun
o'brienianum	24–62	red, pink, orange	1	various	half-sun
prismatocarpum	18–32	vivid yellow striped purple	2–3	summer	full sun
polybulbon	10	brown	1–2	autumn	half-sun
radiatum	12	green and white	1–2	summer	full sun
stamfordianum	15–18	yellow and red	1	spring	half-sun
tampense	24–30	brown and green	½–1	summer	full sun
vitellinum	7–12	cinnabar red	1	winter	dappled sun
GALEANDRA					
devoniana	20–24	brown-pink	3	summer	half-sun
HABENARIA					
radiata	8–40	white	3–4	summer	sun
LAELIA					
anceps	24–30	lavender	4	autumn	
autumnalis	7–12	rose-purple	3–4	autumn	full sun
flava	6–10	canary yellow	1½	various	half-sun
gouldiana	16	lavender	4	autumn	half-sun
harpophylla	16–20	orange	2–3	winter	full sun
pumila	5–9	rose	2–3	summer, autumn	half-sun
purpurata	24–40	rose with brown petals	5–7	summer	full sun
superbiens	36–48	rose and purple streaked	5–6	winter	full sun
LYCASTE					
aromatica	10–16	yellow	2	winter	dappled sun in growth; semishade when leaves fall
cruenta	10–16	yellow	2	winter	dappled sun

Name	Plant size (inches)	Flower color	Flower size (inches)	Time of bloom	Suggested exposure
deppei	16–24	greenish brown spotted red	5	mostly winter	dappled sun in growth; semishade when leaves fall
gigantea	20–30	olive green	6–7	various	dappled sun
skinneri	15–24	whitish rose	6	various	dappled sun
ONCIDIUM					
ampliatum	10–14	bright yellow spotted red	1	early spring	full sun
leucochilum	10–20	yellow-green	1–2	various	half-sun
ornithorynchum	8–20	rose-lilac	$1^1/_2$–2	autumn, winter	half-sun
sarcodes	10–16	chestnut brown and vivid yellow	1	various	dappled sun
splendidum	12–18	yellow barred brown	$1^1/_2$–2	winter, spring	half-sun
wentworthianum	12–20	yellow and brown	1	various	half-sun
Hybrids					
Golden Sunset	4–6	yellow and brown	$^1/_2$–1	winter	half-sun
Missy 'Richella'	4–6	yellow-red	$^1/_2$–1	winter	half-sun
O. Barbie	4–6	red-orange	$^1/_2$–1	winter	half-sun
Seka 'Hot Stuff'	4–6	yellow-brown	$^1/_2$–1	winter	half-sun
'Strawberry Delight'	4–6	white spotted with red	$^1/_2$–1	winter	half-sun
PHAIUS					
grandifolius	22–40	brown and white	4	spring, summer	dappled sun, semishade
maculatus	22–40	buff-yellow marked brown	3	spring	dappled sun, semishade
PHALAENOPSIS (leaf spread)					
amabilis	8–24	white	3–4	winter	semishade
buyssoniana	5–9	crimson, purple, and white	$1^1/_2$	summer	semishade
esmeralda	4–7	pink or lavender	1	various	semishade
leuddemanniana	6–12	white heavily barred with amethyst purple	$1^1/_2$–2	various	semishade
parishii	2–5	white with rose-purple	$^1/_2$–1	summer	semishade
mannii	7–8	golden yellow barred brown	1	various	semishade
rosea	4–8	white with rose-purple	$1^1/_2$	various	semishade
schilleriana	6–16	pink	2–3	winter	dappled sun
stuartiana	5–15	white with brown	2–3	spring	dappled sun

Name	Plant size (inches)	Flower color	Flower size (inches)	Time of bloom	Suggested exposure
PLEIONE					
hookeriana	5–6	rose-purple	3	spring	dappled sun
maculata	10–12	white with white lip streaked purple	2	late autumn	dappled sun
pricei	5–6	pale rose	4	spring	dappled sun
RHYNCOSTYLIS					
gigantea	24–30	white spotted red	3–4	summer	half-sun
retusa	22–30	white spotted purple	2–3	summer	half-sun
SOBRALIA					
decora	20–24	rose	5	summer	full sun
leucoxantha	36–48	rose	7	summer	full sun
micrantua	62–84	rose	6	summer	full sun
SPATHOGLOTTIS					
aurea	24–30	yellow	1	spring	half-sun
plicata	30–36	red	1	spring	half-sun
STANHOPEA					
ecornuta	24–36	white spotted purple	5–7	summer	shade
insignis	24–36	yellow spotted purple	5–7	summer	shade
oculata	24–36	lemon yellow spotted black	5–7	summer	shade
tigrina	24–36	orange blotched with purple	7–8	summer, autumn	shade
wardii	24–36	yellow or white spotted purple	5–6	summer	shade
TRICHOPILIA					
crispa	8–14	cherry with white lip	3–5	spring, summer	half-sun
elegans	7–12	white	2	spring, summer	half-sun
marginata	6–10	pink	5	spring, summer	half-sun
suavis	8–16	white spotted red, pink lip	6	spring, summer	half-sun
tortilis	8–12	whitish pink, white lip	5	spring, summer	half-sun
VANDA					
coerulea	36–60	pale blue	4	autumn, winter	full sun
parishii	24–30	burgundy	4	autumn	full sun
roxburghii	28–32	green and brown	4	winter	full sun
suavis	36–60	white spotted red	4	various	full sun
teres	36–60	pale rose	4	various	full sun

Easy-to-Grow Orchids for the Beginner

Bletia purpurea
Brassavola cucullata, B. nodosa
Brassia caudata, B. gireoudiana, B. maculata
Calanthe rosea, C. vestita
Cattleya citrina, C. forbesii
Cypripedium concolor
Dendrobium aggregatum, D. nobile and hybrids,
    D. pierardii, D. thyrsiflorum
Epidendrum aromaticum, E. atropurpureum, E. fra-
    grans, E. o'brienianum
Lycaste aromatica, L. deppei, L. skinneri
Oncidium apliatum, O. sarcodes, O. splendidum
Phaius grandifolius
Phalaenopsis amabilis, P. esmeralda, P. rosea
Stanhopea oculata, S. wardii
Trichopilia elegans, T. suavis, T. tortilis

Orchid Flowers by Color

White
    Aerides odoratum
    Brassavola glauca
    Cypripedium niveum
    Phalaenopsis amabilis
    Trichopilia elegans

Lavender
    Bletia purpurea
    Cattleya skinneri
    Dendrobium pierardii
    Dendrobium superbum
    Laelia pumila
    Laelia superbiens
    Oncidium ornithorynchum

Phalaenopsis esmeralda
Phalaenopsis rosea
Pleione hookeriana

Yellow
    Dendrobium aggregatum
    Dendrobium chrysotoxum
    Epidendrum prismatocarpum
    Laelia flava
    Oncidium ampliatum
    Oncidium splendidum

Red
    Epidendrum vitellinum
    Epidendrum o'brienianum

Orchid Flowers by Seasons

Spring
    Cattleya skinneri
    Dendrobium aggregatum
    Dendrobium chrysotoxum
    Dendrobium pierardii
    Epidendrum aromaticum
    Epidendrum atropurpureum
    Oncidium ampliatum
    Trichopilia suavis

Summer
    Brassia maculata
    Calanthe biloba
    Calanthe masuca
    Cattleya aclandiae
    Cattleya citrina
    Cattleya forbesii
    Stanhopea oculata
    Stanhopea wardii

Autumn
  Cypripedium insigne
  Cypripedium villosum
  Epidendrum vitellinum
  Laelia autumnalis
  Oncidium ornithorynchum
  Phalaenopsis amabilis
  Pleione maculata

Winter
  Calanthe rosea
  Calanthe vestita
  Epidendrum elegans
  Laelia superbiens
  Oncidium splendidum
  Vanda coerulea

Orchid Types

Single-flowered (One flower to a stem,
but sometimes two or more stems in bloom
at the same time)
  Cattleya citrina
  Laelia pumila
  Lycaste aromatica
  Lycaste deppei
  Lycaste gigantea
  Lycaste skinneri
  Miltonia spectabilis
  Pleione hookeriana
  Pleione maculata

Spray orchids
  Calanthe vestita
  Dendrobium aggregatum
  Epidendrum aromaticum
  Epidendrum stamfordianum

Oncidium ampliatum
Oncidium leucochilum
Oncidium ornithorynchum
Oncidium sarcodes
Oncidium splendidum
Oncidium wentworthianum
Phalaenopsis amabilis
Vanda coerulea

Cluster-flowering
  Brassavola glauca
  Cattleya skinneri
  Dendrobium chrysotoxum
  Dendrobium thyrsiflorum
  Epidendrum o'brienianum
  Laelia superbiens
  Phaius grandifolius

Pendant orchids
  Aerides crassifolium
  Aerides multiflorum
  Aerides odoratum
  Brassia maculata
  Dendrobium pierardii
  Dendrobium superbum

Plant Location

Warm location
  Aerides fieldingii
  Aerides odoratum
  Brassia maculata
  Cattleya skinneri
  Dendrobium chrysotoxum
  Oncidium splendidum
  Phalaenopsis amabilis
  Stanhopea oculata

Stanhopea tigrina
Stanhopea wardii
Vanda suavis
Vanda teres

Full sun
Aerides fieldingii
Aerides odoratum
Brassavola cucullata
Brassavola digbyana
Brassavola nodosa
Brassia maculata
Dendrobium aggregatum
Dendrobium chrysotoxum
Epidendrum aromaticum
Epidendrum atropurpureum
Epidendrum prismatocarpum
Laelia superbiens
Oncidium ampliatum
Vanda suavis
Vanda teres

Cold location
Cattleya citrina
Cypripedium fairrieanum
Cypripedium villosum
Epidendrum vitellinum
Laelia autumnalis
Laelia superbiens
Miltonia vexillaria
Pleione hookeriana
Pleione maculata
Vanda coerulea

Shaded window
Cypripedium bellatum
Cypripedium insigne
Epidendrum vitellinum
Phalaenopsis amabilis
Phalaenopsis lueddemanniana
Stanhopea oculata
Stanhopea tigrina
Stanhopea wardii

United States Orchid Suppliers

The inclusion of an orchid mail order source does not constitute an endorsement for that company. Nor are all companies represented here.

Alberts & Merkel Bros., Inc.
2210 South Federal Highway
Boynton Beach, FL 33435
Orchid list: $1

The Angraecum House
P.O. Box 976
Grass Valley, CA 95945
Madagascan and other African species
Write for information

Arm-Roy
3376 Foothill Road
P.O. Box 385
Carpinteria, CA 93013
Species, hybrids

Bastrop Tropicals
Box 628
Bastrop, TX 78602
Botanicals

Bates Orchids, Inc.
7911 U.S. Highway 301
Ellenton, FL 33532-3599
Species

John Berryman Orchids
1393 U.S. Route 17
Tabb, VA 23602
Cattleyas, Phalaenopses

Blueberry Hill Orchids
12 Charles Street
Lexington, MA 02173
Phalaenopses; lists available

Bo-Mar Orchids
P.O. Box 6713
San Bernardino, CA 92412
Cattleyas
Seedling, flask list: $1

Carter & Holmes, Inc.
1 Old Mendenhall Road
P.O. Box 608
Newberry, SC 29108
All kinds of orchids
Free list

La Casa Verde
35601 SW 192nd Avenue
Homestead, FL 33034
All types; free price list

Chester Hills Orchids
962 Catfish Lane
Pottstown, PA 19464
Phalaenopses; write for lists

Chula Orchids
230 Chula Vista Street
Chula Vista, CA 92010
Hybrids, species; free lists

Clark Day Orchids
1911 South Bloomfield
Cerritos, CA 90701
Odontoglossums

Drago Orchid Corp.
4601 SW 127th Avenue
Miami, FL 33175
Cattleya species; free list

Evon Orchids
Box 17396
San Diego, CA 92117
Seedlings, mature plants
Free lists

John Ewing Orchids, Inc.
P.O. Box 384
Aptos, CA 95003
Phalaenopsis; free catalogs

Exotics Hawaii Limited
1344 Hoakoa Place
Honolulu, HI 96821
*Cattleyas, Dendrobiums, Vandas,
Oncidiums, and others; no catalogs
or price list; send SASE for
further inquiries*

E-Z Orchids
Box 209
Berwyn, PA 19312
Phalaenopsis, Cattleyas; free lists

Fennell's Orchid Jungle
26715 SW 157th Avenue
Homestead, FL 33031
Cattleyas

Finck Floral Co.
9849-A Kimker Lane
St. Louis, MO 63127-1500
*Cattleyas, species orchids
Free lists on request*

Fordyce Orchids
7259 Tina Place
Dublin, CA 94568
*Miniature Cattleyas
By appointment*

Fort Caroline Orchids
13142 Fort Caroline Road
Jacksonville, FL 32225
Species, Brassias, hybrids

The Garden District
6525 Washington Street
Vintage 1870
Yountville, CA 94599
All kinds; no lists or catalogs

Great Lakes Orchids
28805 Pennsylvania Road
Romulus, MI 48174
Species; write for list

Hartmann's Orchid Lab
424 NE 28th Road
Boca Raton, FL 33431
Phalaenopsis

Hausermann Orchids
2 N 134 Addison Road
Villa Park, IL 60181
Catalog available; large selection

Spencer M. Howard Orchid
Imports
11802 Huston Street
North Hollywood, CA 91607
Species; send SASE for price list

Huan Bui Orchids, Inc.
6900 SW 102nd Avenue
Miami, FL 33173
*Seedlings, clones
Catalog: $2*

Islander Delights Orchids
14568 Twin Peaks Road
Poway, CA 92064
*Oncidiums, Dendrobiums, Vandas
Free list*

J & L Orchids
20 Sherwood Road
Easton, CT 06612
All kinds; free catalog

J.E.M. Orchids
4996 NE Fourth Avenue
Boca Raton, FL 33430
*Miniature Cattleyas, Oncidiums,
   intergenerics*

Jemmco Flowers
Box 23
St. George, SC 29477

Jenetta Nursery
3724 School Road
P.O. Box 298
Fresno, TX 77545
Different varieties

Kaoru Oka Orchids
1346 Wilhelmina Rise
Honolulu, HI 96816
Cattleyas; free list

Kensington Orchids, Inc.
3301 Plyers Mill Road
Kensington, MD 20795
Cattleyas, species

Arnold J. Klemm, Grower
2 E. Algonquin Road
Arlington Heights, IL 60005
Phalaenopsis; free list

Krull-Smith Orchids
Ponkan Road, Route 3, Box 18A
Apopka, FL 32703
Cattleyas, Phalaenopsis

Lauralin Orchids
Route 6, Box 1290B
Mocksville, NC 27208
*Miniatures, species
List on request*

Laurel Orchids
18205 SW 157th Avenue
Miami, FL 33187
Species, seedlings; free catalog

Lines Orchids
1823 Taft Highway
Signal Mountain, TN 37377
*Seedlings, flowering plants,
Cattleya orchids
No catalog*

Lynette Greenhouses
4345 Rogers Lake Road
Kannapolis, NC 28081
Cattleyas

Madcap Orchids
Route 29, Box 391-UU
Fort Myers, FL 33905

Maka Koa Corporation
Box 411
Haleiwa, HI 96712
Cattleyas

Ann Mann
Route 3, Box 202
Orlando, FL 32811
Ascocendas, Vandas; catalog

Maxwell Company
P.O. Box 13141
Fresno, CA 93794
Hybrids; lists available

McClains' Orchid Range
6237 Blanding Boulevard
Jacksonville, FL 32244
Miniature and small-growing plants

Rod McLellan Co.
1450 El Camino Real
San Francisco, CA 94080
Oncidiums, Cattleyas; catalog: $.50

Merryl's
Division of Miah, Inc.
6660 Busch Boulevard
Columbus, OH 43229
Miniatures; send SASE for free list

Mobile Bay Orchids
Route 1, Box 166-D
Mobile, AL 36605
Various; write for free list

Muses' Orchids
3710 North Orchid Drive
Haines City, FL 33844
Seedlings, mature plants; free list

Oak Hill Gardens
P.O. Box 25
Dundee, IL 60118
Species, hybrids; free catalog

The Orchid Center
Highway 17, Box 116
Arcadia, FL 33821
Free catalog

The Orchid House
1699 Sage Avenue
Los Osos, CA 93402
Phalaenopses; no lists

Orchid Species Specialties
P.O. Box 1003
Arcadia, CA 91006
Species; list: $1

Orchid World International
11295 SW 93rd Street
Miami, FL 33176
Cattleyas, Oncidiums, others

Orchidland
920 Homer Road
Woodstock, GA 30188
Phalaenopses

Orchids Bountiful
826 West 3800 South
Bountiful, UT 84010
Species

Orchids by Hausermann, Inc.
2N134 Addison Road
Villa Park, IL 60181
All orchids

Orchids Ltd.
407 E. Carson Street
Carson, CA 90745
Jungle-collected plants

Owens Orchids
P.O. Box 365
Pisgah Forest, NC 28768
Miniature and compact Cattleyas

Paradise of Orchids
1608 Waterline Road
Bradenton, FL 34202
Vandaceous orchid specialists

Pearl Harbor Orchids
99-007 Kealakaha Drive
Aiea, HI 96701

Peninsula Hybrids
635 Marion Avenue
Palo Alto, CA 94301
Hybrids and species

Quality Orchids
P.O. Box 4472
Hialeah, FL 33014
Send for list

R. F. Orchids
28100 SW 182nd Avenue
Homestead, FL 33030
Vandas, Ascocendas; list available

J.R. Rands Orchids
15322 Mulholland Drive
Los Angeles, CA 90077
Cattleyas, species

Joseph R. Redlinger Orchids
9236 SW 57th Avenue
Miami, FL 33156
Cattleyas

Ridgeway Orchid Gardens
2467 Ridgeway Drive
National City, CA 92050
Phalaenopses

Riverbend Orchids
Route 1, Box 590E
Biloxi, MS 39532
Hybrids; free list

Rubin In Orchids
15200 SW 46th Street
Miami, FL 33175
Meristems; list on request

Seagulls Landing Orchids
P.O. Box 388
Glen Head, NY 11545
Miniature Cattleyas; free catalog

Stewart Orchids, Inc.
1212 E. Las Tunas Drive
P.O. Box 307
San Gabriel, CA 91778
Cattleyas, miniature Cattleyas

Su-An Nursery
58 Kirklees Road
Pittsford, NY 14534
Phalaenopses, Cattleyas
Free catalog on request

Sunswept Laboratories
P.O. Box 1913
Studio City, CA 91604
Phalaenopses, orchid seed sowing, micro-
propagation

Tammany Tropicals Unlimited, Inc.
760 North Causeway Boulevard
Mandeville, LA 70448
Phalaenopses; send SASE for current
price list

Trymwood Orchids
2500 Rockdell Street
La Crescenta, CA 91214
Colored Cattleyas; flask list available

J. Milton Warne
260 Jack Lane
Honolulu, HI 96817
Hybrids; no catalog

Ken West Orchids
P.O. Box 1332
Pahoa, HI 96778

Wilk Orchid Specialties
P.O. Box 1177
Kaneohe, HI 96744
Assorted orchids; no catalog

Yamamoto Dendrobiums Hawaii
P.O. Box 1003
Arcadia, CA 91006
Species; list: $1

Yardley Orchids
1225 Madison Drive
Yardley, PA 19067
Phalaenopses

Zuma Canyon Orchids, Inc.
5949 Bonsall Drive
Malibu, CA 90265
Phalaenopses; free list

International Orchid Suppliers

Importation of orchids from foreign lands such as Honduras, Taiwan, and others is under strict rules of the CITES regulations and it is best to order from U.S. orchid growers rather than import orchids. The British Orchid Growers Association holds its annual show every March at the Royal Horticultural Society Hall, Vincent Square, Westminster, London.

The Bangkrabue Nursery
174 Ruam Chit Lane
Amnuai Songkhram Road
P.O. Box 3-150
Bangkok 3, Thailand 10 300
Orchids of Thailand; free list

Bardfield Orchids
Great Bardfield
Braintree
Essex CM7 4RZ
United Kingdom
Open Saturdays and Mondays only

Burnham Nurseries Ltd.
5 Orchid Avenue
Kingsington
Newton Abbot
Devon TQ12 3HG
United Kingdom
Mail order; wholesale

Caribe Orchid Growers
P.O. Box 26
Carolina, Puerto Rico 00628
Species

Green Orchids Company
P.O. Box 7-587
Taipei, Taiwan, R.O.C.
Cattleyas

Ivens Orchids Ltd.
St. Albans Road
Sandridge
Herts. AL4 9LB
United Kingdom
Wholesale

Kabukiran Orchids
81 Maginoo Street
P.O. Box 7744 ADC
Quezon City, Philippines
Philippine orchids; list: $1

E. G. Kamm
Valle de Angeles, F.M.
Honduras
Species; free price list

A. J. Keeling & Son
Grange Nurseries
Westgate Hill
Bradford
Yorkshire
United Kingdom

Keith Andrew Orchids Ltd.
Plush
Dorchester
Dorset DT2 7RH
United Kingdom
Mail order; wholesale

Lipanda Orchids
The Vandas
Sidbury
Bridgnorth
Shropshire WV16 6PY
United Kingdom
Mail order; wholesale

Mansell & Hatcher Ltd.
Cragg Wood Nurseries
Rawdon
Leeds LS19 6LQ
United Kingdom
Mail order; wholesale

Marcel Lecoufle
5 rue de Paris
94470 Boissy-St. Léger
France
Catalog, list on request

McBeans Orchids Ltd.
Coolsbridge
Lewes
Sussex
United Kingdom
Mail order; wholesale

Nurseryman's Haven
Kalimpong 734301
India
*Indo-Burmese, Himalayan orchids;
free list*

Ratcliffe Orchids Ltd.
Chilton
Didcot
Oxon OX11 ORT
United Kingdom
Mail order; wholesale

Royden Orchids
Perks Lane
Prestwood
Great Missenden
Bucks
United Kingdom

St. Dunstan's Nursery
Ham Street
Baltonsborough
Glastonbury
Somerset
United Kingdom

David Stead Orchids
Leeds Road Nurseries
Lofthouse
Wakefield
West Yorkshire
United Kingdom

Sukhakul Nursery
15 Klahom Lane
P.O. Box 3-97
Bangkrabue
Bangkok 3
Thailand
Thai orchid species; free list

T. Orchids
77/3 Chaengwattana Road
Pak-kred Nonthaburi, Thailand
P.O. Box 21-19
Bangkok
Thailand
*Vandas, Ascocendas, Dendrobiums
Catalog and price list: $5*

Vacherot & Lecoufle
30 rue de Valenton, BP8
94470 Boissy-St. Léger
France
All genera; color catalog: $2

Wellbank Orchids
Pardon
Oakley
Hants. RG23 7DY
United Kingdom
Mail order

Equipment Suppliers and Book Dealers

The Backdoor Pottery
P.O. Box 981
Ingram, TX 78025
Orchid pots

Clarel Laboratories, Inc.
513 Grove
Deerfield, IL 60015
Orchid food; free catalog

Day's
4725 NW 36th Avenue
Miami, FL 33142
Tier plant benches; free brochures

Environmental Concepts
710 NW 57th Street
Fort Lauderdale, FL 33309
Light-intensity meters

Finck Floral Co.
9849-A Kimker Lane
St. Louis, MO 63127
Orchid food

H. G. Hees
99A Kiln Ride
Wokingham, Berkshire RG11 3PD
*Books, composts, culture media,
plant food, equipment*

Hydrofarm
150 Bellam Boulevard, Suite 300-A0
San Rafael, CA 94901
Lighting supplies; free catalog

Idle Hours Orchids
905 SW Coconut Drive
Fort Lauderdale, FL 33315
Servo orchid potting mix

Indoor Gardening Supplies
P.O. Box 40567AO
Detroit, MI 48240
*Plant stands, lamps, accessories
Free catalog*

Keiki Grow, Dr. James D. Brasch
Box 354, McMaster University
Hamilton, Ontario L8S lC0 Canada
Plant hormones

B. D. Lynn
1438 West Valerio Street
Santa Barbara, CA 93101
Orchids in gold (jewelry)

Don Mattern
267 Filbert Street
San Francisco, CA 94133
Humidifiers for greenhouses

McQuerry Orchid Books
Mary Noble McQuerry
5700 West Salerno Road
Jacksonville, FL 32244
Rare, old, and new books

Ofiduca International, Inc.
P.O. Box 161302
Miami, FL 33116
*Potting mediums
Free catalog*

Orchid Art Gallery
1765 Victory Boulevard
Staten Island, NY 10314
Indoor greenhouses

Orchid Lovers' Sales Directory &
   Guide to Regional Sources
P.O. Box 17125
Rochester, NY 14617
*Regional guidebook to orchid societies;
   write for price*

Pacific Coast Greenhouse Mfg. Co.
8360 Industrial Avenue
Cotati, CA 94928
Humidifiers; free brochures and price list

Silvaperl Products Ltd.
P.O. Box 8
Harrogate, North Yorks. HG2 8JW
Growing media

Spiral Filtration, Inc.
747 North Twin Oaks Valley Rd.
San Marcos, CA 92069
Water-purification system
Catalog: $5

Tropical Plant Products, Inc.
P.O. Box 7754
Orlando, FL 32854
Tree fern products, potting
  mediums, fertilizers, wire goods

Twin Oak Books
4343 Causeway Drive
Lowell, MI 49331
Orchid books (vast selection)

C. H. Whitehouse Ltd.
Buckhurst Works
Frant, Sussex TN3 9BN
All-cedar orchid houses, ventilation and
  heating equipment

Yonah Manufacturing Co.
P.O. Box 280 AO
Cornelia, GA 30531
Shade cloth
Free informational kit

Orchid Societies and Periodicals

Membership in any society listed here includes the society's worthwhile publication.

United States

The American Orchid Society
The American Orchid Society Bulletin
6000 South Olive Street
West Palm Beach, FL 33405
$30/yr.; published monthly

The Orchid Digest Corporation
The Orchid Digest
c/o Mrs. Norman H. Atkinson
P.O. Box 916
Carmichael, CA 95609-0916
$18/yr.; published bimonthly

South Florida Orchid Society
The Florida Orchidist
13300 SW 111th Avenue
Miami, FL 33176
$12/yr.; published quarterly

International

Australian Orchid Review
Sydney Mail Exchange
Australia 2012
Published quarterly

The Orchid Review
5 Orchid Avenue
Kingsington
Newton Abbot, Devon TQ 12 3HG
United Kingdom
Published monthly

South African Orchid Journal
c/o Hugh Rogers, editor
10 Somers Road
Clarendon
Pietermaritzburg 3201, South Africa
Published quarterly

Glossary

aerial roots   roots growing outside the potting mix or hanging free in the air

anther   the part of the stamen that contains pollen

asexual   describes propagation by division and meristem

axil   the upper angle between a stem or branch and a leaf

backbulb   the older pseudobulbs behind the growing lead

bifoliate   having two leaves

bigeneric   involving two genera in the parentage of a plant

bisexual   two-sexed; the flowers possess both stamens and pistils

botanical   refers to species not grown for cut flowers

bract   a leaflike sheath near the base of the flower stem

bulb   plant structure for storage purposes, usually underground; generally includes corms, rhizomes, and tubers as well as true bulbs

bulbous   having the shape and character of a bulb

calyx   outer circle of floral parts, usually green

chlorotic   excessive yellowing from the breaking down of chlorophyll

chromosomes   structures within the cell nucleus that carry the genes

clone   a sexually produced, seed-grown individual and all its subsequent asexual (vegetative) propagations

column   the central body of the orchid flower, formed by the union of the stamens and pistil

compost   decomposed vegetable matter

cultivar   plant form originating in cultivation

cutting   vegetative plant part capable of producing an identical plant

deciduous   describes plants that lose leaves at maturity in certain seasons

diploid   orchid with the normal number of chromosomes

division   the means by which a single cultivar is divided into two or more plants

dormancy   resting, a period of inactivity when plants grow less or not at all

dorsal   pertaining to the back or outer surface

epiphyte   a plant that grows on another plant but is not a parasite because it obtains its nourishment from the air

eye   the bud of a growth

family   a group of related genera

force   to make a plant grow or bloom ahead of its natural season

gene   the unit of inheritance, located at a specific site on a chromosome

genetics   the study of heredity and variation

genus   a subdivision of a family, consisting of one or more species that show similar characteristics and appear to have a common ancestry

germination   process of seed sprouting

grex   the named cross between two different orchids

habitat   the locality in which a plant normally grows

hirsute   pubescent, the hairs being coarse and stiff

hybrid   the offspring resulting from the cross between two different species or hybrids

indigenous   native; not introduced

inflorescence   the flowering part of a plant

intergeneric   between or among two or more genera

internode   the part of a stem between two nodes

keiki   a plantlet produced as an offset or offshoot from another plant—a Hawaiian term orchidists use

labellum   the lip, or modified petal, of an orchid flower

lateral   of or pertaining to the side of an organ

lead   a new vegetative growth

leaflet   segment of a compound leaf

leaf mold   decayed or decomposed leaves, useful in potting mixes

linear   long and narrow, with parallel margins

lip   the labellum, usually quite different from the other two petals

lithophyte   a plant that grows on rocks

mericlone   a plant produced by meristem culture

meristem   the quickly developing plant tissue at the point of growth

meristem culture   describing clonal propagation of plants

monopodial   growing only from the apex of the plant

mutation   a departure from the parent type; a sport

natural hybrid   a hybrid produced by chance in the wild

node   a joint on a stem where a bud or leaf is attached

nomenclature   a system of names or naming

offset   a plantlet that may form at the base of an orchid or on the stem, pseudobulb, or inflorescence

parasite   a plant that lives on and derives part or all of its nourishment from another plant

petal   one of the three inner segments of an orchid flower, not modified to form the lip

petiole   supporting stalk of a leaf

pinnate   leaf form, like a feather, with sections arranged along the sides of the leaf stalk

pistil   the seed-bearing organ of a flower, consisting of the stigma, style, and ovary

plicate   pleated or folded like a fan

pollen   the fertilizing grains borne by the anther

pollination   the transfer of pollen from the anther to the stigma

polyploid   containing one or more additional sets of chromosomes beyond the normal diploid number

potbound   condition of a plant when a mat of roots fills the container

protocorm   a tuberlike structure formed in the early stages of a plant's development

pseudobulb   the thickened portion of a stem, but not a true bulb

quadrigeneric   pertaining to four genera

raceme   a simple inflorescence of stalked flowers

rhizome   a root-bearing horizontal stem that, in orchids, usually lies on or just beneath the ground surface

rosette   a cluster of leaves arranged around a short stem

saccate   pouched or baglike

scape   a flower stalk without leaves, arising directly from the ground

self-pollination   the pollination of a flower by its own pollen

semiterete   semicircular in cross section; semicylindrical

sepal   one of the three outer segments of an orchid flower

sheath   a tubular envelope protecting the developing buds or stems

species   a group of plants sharing one or more common characteristics

sphagnum moss   bog material dried and used alone as a planting medium or in a mixture

spike   a flower stem

sport   a deviation from the usual form; a mutation

spur   a hollow, tubular extension of the lip

stamen   the male organ of a flower, bearing the pollen

stigma   the part of the pistil that is receptive to the pollen

stolon   creeping, horizontal stem usually producing a new plant at the tip

style   the part of the pistil bearing the stigma

succulent   type of plant that stores moisture in stems or leaves

symbiosis   the close association of dissimilar organisms, with benefits to both

sympodial   form of growth in which each new shoot, arising from the rhizome of previous growth, is a complete plant in itself

Glossary

taxonomist   scientific specialist concerned with organism classification and names

terete   circular in cross section; cylindrical

terrestrial   growing in or on the ground

tetraploid   plant cells with four times the normal number of chromosomes, compared to common species having a diploid number of chromosomes

transpiration   loss of water from the plant tissue by evaporation

tribe   a group of related genera

trigeneric   pertaining to three genera

tuber   a thickened, normally underground stem

umbel   flat or ball-shaped flower cluster

unifoliate   having one leaf

unilateral   arranged only on one side

unisexual   having flowers of one sex only

vandaceous   refers to Vanda genus and to other plants that similarly have a monopodial type of growth

vegetative propagation   the increasing of a particular plant by division, offset, keiki, etc.

virus   an infectious agent that increases in living cells, causing disease

Bibliography

Some of the books in this list are out of print but can be secured through antiquarian book dealers or found in libraries.

Ames, Blanche. *Drawings of Florida Orchids*, 2nd ed. Explanatory notes by Oakes Ames. Cambridge, MA: Botanical Museum of Harvard University, 1959.

_____, and Donovan S. Correll. *Orchids of Guatemala*. Chicago: Field Museum of Natural History, 1952–1953. (Fieldiana: *Botany*, vol. 26, nos. 1 and 2.) Supplement by Correll, 1966. 2 vols., 726 pp.

Blowers, John. *Pictorial Orchid Growing*. Maidstone, Kent, England: John W. Blowers, 96 Marion Crescent, 1966. 128 pp.

Cady, Leo, and T. Rotherham. *Australian Orchids in Color*. Sydney: Reed, 1970. 50 text pp., 107 color plates.

Chittenden, Fred J. *Dictionary of Gardening*. Oxford, England: Clarendon Press, 1951, 1956, 1965. 4 vols.

Correll, Donovan S. *Native Orchids of North America, North of Mexico*. New York: Ronald, 1950. 400 pp.

Craighead, Frank S. *Orchids and Other Air Plants of the Everglades National Park*. Coral Gables, FL: University of Miami Press, 1963. 125 pp.

Dodson, Calaway H., and Robert J. Gillespie. *The History of the Orchids*. Nashville: Mid-America Orchid Congress, 1967. 158 pp.

Dunsterville, G. C. K. *Introduction to the World of Orchids*. Garden City, NY: Doubleday, 1964. 104 pp.

Fennell, T. A., Jr. *Orchids for Home and Garden*. New York: Rinehart, 1956; rev. ed., 1959.

Garrard, Jeanne. *Growing Orchids for Pleasure*. South Brunswick, NJ: Barnes, 1966. 302 pp.

Ghose, B. N. *Beautiful Indian Orchids*. Darjeeling, India: Ghose, 1959; 2nd ed., 1969. 155 pp.

Graf, Alfred Byrd. *Exotica 3: Pictorial Cyclopedia of Exotic Plants*. Rutherford, NJ: Roehrs, 1963. 1,828 pp., 901 illustrations and descriptions of orchids.

Grubb, Roy, and Ann Grubb. *Selected Orchidaceous Plants*. Parts 1–3. Caterham, Surrey, England: Roy and Ann Grubb, 62 Chaldon Common Rd., 1961–1963. Drawn and hand-printed by the authors. Harvard University Botanical Museum Leaflets. By subscription, or available separately from the American Orchid Society, 6000 South Olive St., West Palm Beach, FL 33405.

Hawkes, Alex D. *Encyclopedia of Cultivated Orchids*. London: Faber & Faber, 1965. 602 pp.

_____. *Orchids: Their Botany and Culture.* New York: Harper & Row, 1961. 297 pp.

Kramer, Jack. *Growing Orchids at Your Windows.* New York: Van Nostrand, 1963. 151 pp.

_____. *The World Wildlife Fund Book of Orchids.* New York: Abbeville, 1989. 276 pp.

Moulen, Fred. *Orchids in Australia.* Sydney: Australia Edita, 1958. 149 pp., 100 color figures.

Noble, Mary. *You Can Grow Cattleya Orchids.* Jacksonville, FL: Mary Noble, 3003 Riverside Ave., 1968. 148 pp.

Northern, Rebecca Tyson. *Orchids as House Plants.* 2nd rev. ed. New York: 1955, 1976.

Oca, Rafael Montes de. *Hummingbirds and Orchids of Mexico.* Mexico City: Fournier, 1963. 158 pp., reproductions of watercolors.

Richter, Walter. *The Orchid World.* New York: 1965. 280 pp., 64 color plates. Revised and translated from 1958 edition.

Sander, David. *Orchids and Their Cultivation,* rev. ed. London: Blandford, 1962. 183 pp.

Sander, Fred. *Reichenbachia: Orchids Illustrated and Described.* 4 vols. London: 1888–1894. The plates are collectors' items.

Sander & Sons. *Complete List of Orchid Hybrids.* St. Albans, England: Sanders, 1946. Addenda, 3 vols., 1946–1948, 1949–1951, 1952–1954.

_____. *One-Table List of Orchid Hybrids, 1946–1960.* 2 vols. St. Albans, England: Sanders, 1961. Addenda, 1963, 1966.

_____. *Sander's Orchid Guide.* Rev. ed. St. Albans, England: Sanders, 1927. 451 pp.

_____. *Sander's List of Orchid Hybrids.* London: Royal Horticultural Society. Addenda, 1961–1970, 1971–1975, 1976–1980. Also available from the American Orchid Society, 6000 South Olive Street, West Palm Beach, FL 33405.

Schelpe, E. A. C. L. E. *An Introduction to the South African Orchids.* London: Macdonald, 1966. 109 pp.

Schweinfurth, Charles. *Orchids of Peru.* 4 vols. Chicago: Field Museum of Natural History, 1958–1961. (*Fieldiana: Botany,* vol. 30, nos. 1–4.) 1,005 pp.

Veitch, James & Sons. *A Manual of Orchidaceous Plants.* 4 vols. Reprint. Amsterdam: Ashler, 1963.

Watkins, John V. *ABCs of Orchid Growing.* 3rd ed. Englewood Cliffs, NJ: Prentice-Hall, 1956. 190 pp.

White, E. A. *American Orchid Culture,* rev. ed. New York: De la Mare, 1942.

Williams, John G., and Andrew E. Williams. *Field Guide to Orchids of North America.* New York: Universe Books, 1983. Illustrated by Norma Arlott. 144 pp.

Williams, Louis O. *The Orchidaceae of Mexico.* Tegucigalpa, Honduras: Escuela Agricola Panamericana, 1952. (*Cieba,* vol. 2, in 4 parts.)

Withner, Carl L. *The Orchids: A Scientific Survey.* New York: Ronald, 1959. 648 pp.

Index